NOT SO MERRY WAKEFIELD

Aspects of Wakefield 2, Kate Taylor
ISBN: 1-871647-68-1
192pp. Illustrated. £9.95

Aspects of Wakefield 3, Kate Taylor
ISBN: 1-903425-06-9
192pp. Illustrated. £9.99

Aspects of Leeds 2, Lynn Stevenson Tate
ISBN: 1-871647-59-2
176pp. Illustrated. £9.95

Aspects of Leeds 3, Lynn Stevenson Tate
ISBN: 1-903425-05-0
192pp. Illustrated. £9.99

Aspects of Barnsley 7, Brian Elliott
ISBN: 1-903425-24-7
192pp. Illustrated. £9.99

The Making of Leeds, David Goodman
ISBN: 1-903425-41-7
176pp. Illustrated. £9.99

The Making of Sheffield, Mel Jones
ISBN: 1-903425-42-5
176pp. Illustrated. £9.99

The Making of Barnsley, Brian Elliott
ISBN: 1-903425-90-5
192pp. Illustrated. £9.99

The Making of the West Yorkshire Landscape, Anthony Silsden
ISBN: 1-903425-31-X
128pp. Illustrated. £9.99

The Making of the South Yorkshire Landscape, Mel Jones
ISBN: 1-871647-75-4
128pp. Illustrated. £9.99

The Making of Huddersfield, George Redmonds
ISBN: 1-903425-39-5
176pp. Illustrated. £9.99

Foul Deeds and Suspicious Deaths in Leeds, David Goodman
ISBN: 1-903425-08-5
160pp. Illustrated. £9.99

Foul Deeds and Suspicious Deaths around Pontefract and Castleford, Keith Henson
ISBN: 1-903425-54-9
176pp. Illustrated. £9.99

Foul Deeds and Suspicious Deaths in Wakefield, Kate Taylor
ISBN: 1-903425-07-7
176pp. Illustrated. £9.99

More Foul Deeds and Suspicious Deaths in Wakefield, Kate Taylor
ISBN: 1-903425-48-4
176pp. Illustrated £9.99

Yorkshire Mining Veterans, Brian Elliott
ISBN: 1-903425-58-1
176pp. Illustrated £9.99

Please contact us via any of the methods below for more information or a catalogue.
WHARNCLIFFE BOOKS
47 Church Street – Barnsley – South Yorkshire – S70 2AS
Tel: 01226 734555 – 734222 Fax: 01226 734438
E-mail: enquiries@pen-and-sword.co.uk – Website: www.wharncliffebooks.co.uk

Not So Merry

WAKEFIELD

Kate Taylor

Series Editor
Brian Elliott

Wharncliffe Books

First Published in Great Britain in 2005 by
Wharncliffe Books
an imprint of
Pen and Sword Books Ltd
47 Church Street
Barnsley
South Yorkshire
S70 2AS

Copyright © Kate Taylor, 2005

ISBN: 1-903425-72-7

Typeset in 10/12pt Plantin by Mac Style Ltd, Scarborough.

Printed and bound in England by
CPI UK.

Pen and Sword Books Ltd incorporates the Imprints of
Pen & Sword Aviation, Pen & Sword Maritime,
Pen & Sword Military, Wharncliffe Books
Pen & Sword Select, Pen and Sword Military Classics
and Leo Cooper.

For a complete list of Pen & Sword titles please contact
PEN & SWORD BOOKS LIMITED
47 Church Street
Barnsley
South Yorkshire
S70 2BR
England
E-mail: enquiries@pen-and-sword.co.uk
Website: www.pen-and-sword.co.uk

Contents

Westgate in 2005.

Wood Street in 2005.

Quite when or why Wakefield gained the epithet 'Merry' is not known. Certainly the phrase was in use in the eighteenth century. In 1887 it provided the title for a book, *Memories of Merry Wakefield* by the octogenarian Henry Clarkson. Looking back, he saw the 1820s as a period when Wakefield could truly be described as 'merry': Wakefield had its first musical festival in the parish church, there were subscription concerts in the newly-built music saloon, there were assemblies and plays, and private carriages brought the gentry into town from country houses such as Bretton Hall, Chevet Hall, Denby Grange, and Nostell Priory. Clarkson, living through most of the nineteenth century, remarked on the many changes that he had experienced. He spoke of the town's fine new public buildings and its prosperity; the only cloud on the horizon in the 1880s was from the polluting smoke of industry. My own memories, as a septuagenarian, are of a less than merry Wakefield and of the changes of the twentieth century that are, as I see them, largely unwelcome.

As I write more, and very extensive, changes are planned which may be for the better but which will render unfamiliar the Wakefield I have known. There is a massive scheme to redevelop the area of the market, between Brook Street and Teall Street, extending from Westmorland Street to Jacob's Well Lane. It will involve the diversion of Marsh Way and the relocation of the outdoor markets. The second Market Hall, built only in 1964 on the same site as the Victorian one, is now scheduled for demolition. There is to be a new public library, replacing the original one in Drury Lane and the erstwhile County Library Headquarters in Balne Lane. There is to be a regeneration of the waterfront with a new art gallery. However, the future of the most important building there, the Calder and Hebble warehouse of the 1790s, remains unclear.

More plans, this time to redevelop the area between Westgate and Balne Lane, were published in April 2005. Much of the site has been occupied by the Express Dairies milk pasteurising and bottling centre which had opened in 1959 and was at the time the most advanced, technologically, in the world for its purpose. The scheme envisages a new site for Westgate Station, yet another hotel (on Westgate) and more residential and office development. A proposed new road from Westgate to Bell Street could develop into another inner relief road and will certainly entail the demolition of nineteenth century property.

More houses are planned for the premises in Aberford Road, put up for the Bevin Boys during the war, which became a training college for prison officers in 1959 and closed in 2004. Flats and offices are proposed for a derelict site between Doncaster Road and Fall Ing Lock. Flats are proposed, too, for the prominent site at the corner of Ings Road and Denby Dale Road. Wakefield College is considering relocation. Clayton Hospital is likely to close and its buildings to become available for redevelopment. The West Yorkshire Police Service, with disparate premises in Bond Terrace, Laburnum Road, Northgate, Wood Street and at Bishopgarth, has plans to rationalise its location.

This does not claim to be a definitive history of Wakefield over the last seventy years. Rather, as Clarkson's book was, it is an account of aspects of my own life there and of Wakefield itself from a personal perspective. But I hope that it will join *Memories of Merry Wakefield* as a record of a place that both Henry Clarkson and I have known well.

No one could write today about the history of Wakefield without the help of the distinguished historian John Goodchild and I am grateful to him for much advice and information. I must also thank Brian Elliott, the Commissioning Editor at Wharncliffe Books, and the design team at Mac Style.

CHAPTER 1

MY CHILDHOOD IN THE 1930S AND 1940S

Good things were happening in Wakefield in 1933. The new bridge across the River Calder, anticipated since the beginning of the century, was opened by the Mayor, Councillor Walter Emmett, on 1 June, relieving the medieval bridge and Chantry Chapel of traffic. The bridge was blessed by the Bishop of Wakefield, the Very Reverend J B Seaton. Again in June, a mammoth pageant, celebrating the history of Wakefield and the West Riding was held in Clarence Park. At the same time there was an exhibition of the county's industry in the Drill Hall and paintings by Wakefield's leading artists, John Buckler, Louisa Fennell and Thomas Kilby, were displayed in the Town Hall. On 12 July the newly laid-out rose gardens in Thornes Park were opened. Then on 7 September Wakefield's vast Ryburn reservoir, above Ripponden, which had taken eight years to build at a cost of about £1m, was opened by Councillor Charles Hopkinson. It had been designed and supervised by Wakefield's own waterworks engineer, C Clemesha-Smith. In the evening the dam was floodlit by electricity supplied by the Yorkshire Electric Power Company.

Wakefield Bridge, on the left, originated in the 1340s. The bridge on the right was opened in 1933. *The author*

The formal gardens in Thornes Park in 2005. *The author*

Small wonder that at the time 1933 was designated Wakefield's 'Year of Progress'.

The novelist and playwright David Storey, whose home was in Manor Haigh Road and who was more than half a century later to become a good friend, was born on 13 July.

And on 11 August, 1933 I was born at 28 Eastmoor Road. My parents named me Coral. I abandoned the name before I was thirty and became thereafter Kate.

My parents came to Wakefield, to live first in St Mark's Street, from Sheffield in 1932 when my father was appointed as a section engineer for the National Grid. He had married in 1930 on an August day that was so hot it melted the wax orange blossom on my mother's coronet. My elder sister, Paula, had been born in Sheffield a year later. I was the first of the family to be a native of Wakefield.

Wakefield was then a small and compact, but thriving, place with an economy prospering from coalmining, engineering and textiles. It was the county town of the West Riding of Yorkshire and its handsome Court House, built by the West Riding magistrates in

County Hall, Wood Street, built for the West Riding County Council and opened in 1898. *Wakefield Historical Publications*

1810, and County Hall, completed in 1898, were among its noblest buildings. It had become a city in 1888 when the parish church, boasting the tallest spire in Yorkshire, had been elevated to cathedral status as the mother church of the Diocese of Wakefield.

My first home was the handsome terrace house in Eastmoor Road, built about 1905, which my father rented and which was opposite to what was then called the Asylum but was later renamed Stanley Royd Hospital. Like the Court House, the Asylum had been built by the West Riding magistrates – the forerunners of the West Riding County

11

Eastmoor Road in 2005. *The author*

Council. It was their hospital for 'pauper lunatics'. My mother used to recall wheeling me in the pram alongside the hospital railings and feeling nervous of the inmates who were taking exercise on the other side. I was to become a patient there myself in 1959.

Although we moved within a year, the north-eastern part of Wakefield has always felt like home to me and in 1969 I bought my own house in Pinder's Grove, a very short distance from my birthplace and still almost opposite the grounds of Stanley Royd. Stanfeld Ward, where I was treated, can be seen from my kitchen window.

12

What was this National Grid that had brought my father to Wakefield? By the 1920s electricity was becoming the essential source of power, overtaking gas. Homes and businesses in urban areas were supplied by power stations established by local authorities, or independent companies, in the 1890s and early 1900s. But more rural areas still had no access to electricity. And the demands of industry for electrical power were increasing. The task of the National Grid, set up under the Electricity Supply Act of 1926, was to create a web of transmission lines which would conduct surplus electricity from the individual power stations across the country to wherever it was needed. In 1930 its plans for the mid-east England section of the grid were completed with Wakefield right at the heart of four routes. My father was placed in charge of the part of the grid which centred on Wakefield.

Wakefield Corporation had built its own electricity generating station in the 1890s. An Electric Lighting Committee was set up in November 1893 to secure the necessary order from Parliament (obtained in 1894) and to oversee arrangements for borrowing capital (£25,000), securing a consulting engineer, commissioning designs for the plant and implementing them. For much of the 1890s the committee's chairman was Councillor Benjamin Sherwood, owner of the then recently re-built Theatre Royal and Opera House.

Since Wakefield required a sewage works at much the same time as it embarked on its electricity project, a site was purchased on Calder Vale Road, just to the north-east of the railway line, for both schemes.

The sole purpose of the power station, initially, was to provide electricity for lighting, especially street lighting, although in 1895 the Committee had its first enquiry about power for tramways. As the project developed approaches were made to the Committee about lighting some of Wakefield's major institutions: an early request came in 1894 from the churchwardens at Wakefield Cathedral; in 1895 the School Board asked about the cost of providing electricity to its new school in Ings Road; in 1896 the Guardians of the Wakefield Poor Law Union raised the question with the Committee of providing electricity for the new workhouse infirmary and there were discussions too in regard to the projected County Hall in Wood Street. In January 1897 the Trustees of the Methodist West Parade Chapel inquired about electricity and in September that year the fledgling county council were in touch about a new building at the Pauper Lunatic Asylum.

Power was switched on on Saturday 13 November, 1897. It had not come without controversy. The Committee had elected to build an underground substation at the top of Westgate and, whilst digging a large hole, the Corporation decided to kill two birds with one stone and to erect a men's lavatory down there as well. City residents objected and the Midland Bank, with its premises facing the hole, threatened to sue for damages to its property. But the success of the electricity undertaking was manifest when County Hall, which was completed in 1898, was wired for electricity from the outset. The period light switches, in an art nouveau style, remain fascinating and, with their curvaceous naked women, somewhat erotic, features.

The coming of the Grid in the 1930s meant building a switching and coupling plant close to Wakefield Power Station. From here the sixteen generating plants selected for the Grid would be linked. Besides Wakefield they included Blackburn Meadows and Neepsend at Sheffield, Barnsley, the three stations belonging to the Yorkshire Electric Power Company (Barugh which had been built in 1913 with a view to utilising the surplus gas from the Old Silkstone Colliery's

The author's father at the National Grid substation in Wakefield about 1938. *The author's collection*

coke ovens, Ferrybridge and Thornhill), Halifax, Harrogate, Huddersfield and Hull, Bradford, Foss Island at York, Kirkstall (Leeds), Rotherham, and Lincoln.

This plant was my father's domain. He had his own office. It was little more than a hut, standing close to the site of all the transformers and switching gear. I often played there although there was little for children to do except to make doilies, patterning sheets of paper with a hole punch. The switching and coupling plant was low-lying and close to the River Calder. Beside the office, which was on higher ground, was a small boat which was in regular use so that my father could continue the process of re-routing power by 'throwing' heavy switches, even when the site was flooded. Many a time my father came home saturated having managed to capsize the little vessel.

Father was responsible also for maintaining the Grid's power lines in his area and supervised a team of three workmen; he had always to ensure that the line was 'dead' when he sent them to climb a pylon.

Throughout the twentieth century, the open land surrounding Wakefield became increasingly built-up. Land to the east of Dewsbury Road and north of Flanshaw Lane was originally developed in 1908 and was laid out in parallel avenues as the Garden City. The scheme reflected the idealism of a group of Quakers associated with Wakefield's New Scarborough Adult School who wanted to provide cheap plots where working people could build their own homes and enjoy their own gardens. The idea might seem attractive but development was slow. The plots in Poplar Avenue and Oakleigh Avenue were gradually taken up but those in Ashleigh Avenue remained vacant until the 1930s when the Wakefield building magnate George Crook bought all the remaining sites and filled them with identical semi-detached houses for letting.

Friends of my parents, David and Peggy Pearson, took one of these at 2 Ashleigh Avenue. David Pearson, who was a Scot, had come to Wakefield in 1930 as the assistant chief engineer at British Jeffrey Diamond, then one of Wakefield's great engineering companies. A design engineer, he was to oversee the development of simple coal-cutting machinery into sophisticated electronically-controlled power-loaders and to become the company's technical director.

It was the Pearsons who told my parents in 1933 of the plots that were available to buy in nearby Flanshaw Lane, the other side of

The author's parents and sisters Paula and Enid with the author on the right outside the family home in Flanshaw Lane in 1946. *The author's collection*

town from our Eastmoor Road home. And so we moved in October 1934 to our modest detached house at 196 Flanshaw Lane built on land bought by my father from John Archer, the owner of the nearby large house, Flanshaw Lodge who, in turn, had bought it from the Garden City company. Except for the college terms when I was away at university, I lived there for the next thirty-five years. The house had two small living rooms, each about ten by twelve feet, and a small kitchen on the ground floor, with two principal bedrooms and a boxroom, bathroom and separate lavatory upstairs. Paula and I slept in a twin-bedded room made the more cramped by its dark oak wardrobe and dressing table. When we had visitors – and aunts came to stay with remarkable frequency – it fell to my lot as the younger child to sleep on a camp bed in my parents' room whilst the aunt of the day had mine.

Our warmth came from coal fires. There was a small coke-fired boiler in the kitchen which provided hot water. Central heating for homes such as ours was virtually unknown. Normally we had a fire just in the dining room so that this was the hub of family life. Here was the wireless from which we heard the news and *Children's Hour.* Here we ate, played, and in teenage years, did our homework. On Sundays, but only after lunch, we might have a fire in the sitting room. Upstairs, the house was miserably cold. On winter mornings the insides of the windows would be frosted. Going to the lavatory or having a bath were chilly episodes although in the 1950s Father put an electric strip heater in the bathroom. Only when we were ill would a fire be lit in a bedroom. It was, I still think, worth being ill just for that. Going to sleep with the flicker of the flames reflected on the ceiling was bliss.

The coal was delivered in sacks from the back of an open lorry. We had what we called the 'coal-house' built on to the side of the kitchen, its door forming a side to the back porch. I used to be fearful of the deliveries by be-sooted men and the noise of the coal falling from the sacks. I was fearful, too, of the dustbin men with their dirty clothes and strange shouts and the noisy clanking of the metal bins. This was long before the advent of the plastic wheelie bin but in those days, before the modern excesses of packaging, most of our refuse was burned; the bin was just for ashes and the occasional tin.

Then there were the coal miners themselves. Wakefield was surrounded by collieries. The nearest to our home was Manor Haigh, just off Dewsbury Road, and I would sometimes be woken by the sound of the boots of small groups of men as they went home along Flanshaw Lane. We passed the colliery often enough when we walked to the park along Cross Lane. Manor went long ago, in January 1982; its site on Cross Lane is now occupied by houses.

Walking to the park was a regular feature of my childhood. Normally we went to the entrance to Thornes Park in Horbury Road but sometimes we walked along George-a-Green Road to the gate by the rose gardens in Thornes Road. The park was very well maintained in those days. The parks superintendent lived in a house facing the rose gardens and there were uniformed park keepers patrolling the paths. We were rather frightened of them but they also made us feel safe. Usually we walked by the lake and fed the ducks. There were no Canada geese then as there are now, and the mallards were attractive and quite child friendly. On an island in the lake was a temple with a statue – long gone in the neglect of the last half century. The park

The bandstand in Clarence Park in 2005. *The author*

was really three parks – Clarence, Holmfield and Thornes – the two latter created from adjoining estates which were bought by Wakefield Corporation in 1918 and 1919. Clarence Park came rather earlier as a result of voluntary enterprise, primarily by Charles George Milnes Gaskell of Thornes House and the Wakefield Paxton Society. It was opened in 1893. Sometimes we walked as far as Clarence Park where, on Sunday afternoons, you could sit on the hillside and listen to a band playing in the then-handsome bandstand close to Denby Dale Road. It was vandalised long ago.

One of our treats was a cornet of ice-cream from the horse-drawn cart which stood at the park gates. This came from Lumb's Dairy. The rival ice-cream firm, Massarella's, often had a cart close by but we were never allowed to buy ices from it. The Lumbs had been farmers at Agbrigg and the ice-cream business was founded in 1887 as a way of profiting from surplus milk. The ice-cream was made in premises at the top of Haddingley Hill, on the corner of Barnsley Road and Portobello Road. At one time Lumbs pastured their horses near Sandal Castle in the ten-acre field, a legendary spot which was highly popular in times of snow for sledging. The Lumbs expanded to acquire the Bon Bon shop on Denby Dale Road and, in 1979, a

The kiosk of Lumb's Dairy at Haddingley Hill, Wakefield. *Brian Davidson*

shop in Warrengate. However, in November 1992 the firm went into liquidation. Two of its vans were bought by Joe Brandi who continues to trade from them as Lumb's ices.

We walked in other directions than the park. A favourite walk was down Flanshaw Lane towards Alverthorpe and then, alongside rhubarb fields, to come out on Dewsbury Road close to Roundwood Colliery. Wakefield is part of the 'rhubarb triangle' which lies between Wakefield itself, Bradford and Leeds, and includes Carlton, Carr Gate, East Ardsley, Kirkhamgate and Stanley. The principle of 'forcing' rhubarb was discovered early in the nineteenth century and the landscape used to be, and to an extent still is, dotted with the long, low sheds in which, during the depths of winter, rhubarb is encouraged to grow, its stems shooting up but, in the darkness, remaining pink and tender. It was regarded as a winter fruit, a useful addition to the diet when real fruits such as apples, gooseberries, raspberries and plums were out of season. The rhubarb is harvested by candlelight. Before being taken in for 'forcing' the plant is grown outdoors for three years. The Bradford-Leeds-Wakefield area possessed considerable advantages for its cultivation. It needs plenty

Rhubarb sheds at Thornes in 2005. *The author*

of water and the clay subsoils ensured this. It has been said that in the past the smoke-filled atmosphere shielded the plants from the drying heat of the sun. Drainage for the topsoil could be provided easily by applying ash from local industries. Waste from the textile industry could be spread as a manure.

Until 1962 rhubarb used to be taken by special trains to Covent Garden market in London. There are far fewer market gardens in the Wakefield area today and only twelve rhubarb growers. The rhubarb industry declined in the 1970s for a variety of reasons: imported fruit meant that consumers had plenty of choice even in the winter; many of the sheds were old and needed considerable investment to maintain them adequately; growers found it increasingly difficult to find people to do the seasonal picking for a wage they could afford to pay. But rhubarb has had something of a revival as a delicacy since the 1990s when the local authority began to promote it as an interest for tourism.

Two doors from our home was a footpath, or ginnel, running westward, past the end of Ashleigh Avenue, through Oakleigh and Poplar Avenues to Eden Avenue and, in the opposite direction, to the houses in Flanshaw Park built, again, by George Crook. Builders, before the Second World War, were local firms, employed both by the local authority and for private developments. The ubiquitous Barratts Homes, Tarmac, and Wimpey came much later. We always referred to the path as 'going up the Garden City'. It was a gateway to short walks through the other ginnels and avenues.

In my early teens, I went 'up the Garden City' for piano lessons with Alex Green. In his younger days, in the era of silent films, he had been a cinema pianist but had subsequently built up a reputation for private teaching. The lessons were in a small sitting room at 8 Oakleigh Avenue which he called Harmony House. There was just room for a grand piano and its long stool where Green and his pupil sat side by side. He had a way of shifting along the stool until his thighs were touching yours but – at least where I was concerned – he never made any other embarrassing movement. From time to time his wife would look in. He and his wife, Violet (the colour combination of her name always amused me), were Christian Scientists. They did little to proselytise, however, except to dismiss any ailment as simply 'a belief' of an illness. Despite their convictions, or perhaps because of the failure to recognise her own condition, Violet died of cancer. Alex Green 'showcased' his talents by putting on concerts where both he and his pupils performed.

What strange people they were on our part of Flanshaw Lane although each of the householders was in a senior position professionally or in business. Next door to us on one side were the Umplebys. Walter Umpleby worked at Harraps, the mill on Bective Road at the bottom end of Flanshaw Lane which later became Sirdar. The trade name, I am told, reflected the Zulu name for General Kitchener. Walter's wife, Elizabeth, but known as Lizzie, was loud in every way. She had flaming red (surely dyed) hair, a screeching voice and a tendency to rant. My mother detested her. But she was an excellent cook. In those days middle-class wives did not go out to work. They stayed at home, baked, provided regular meals – often a cooked lunch for returning husbands as well as a high tea – washed, cleaned, shopped, fell out with their friends, and visited for gossip. Living with the Umplebys was Mrs Umpleby's brother, Jim Messon. He had served in the First World War and lost a finger. He looked after the garden. I woke up many a morning to the steady chip chip of his hoe which he seemed to ply from dawn until dusk. But his pride was the greenhouse where he grew geraniums and tomatoes. Mrs Umpleby kept up immense fires, in the summer as well as the winter. Her tiny sitting room was always seriously overheated. Both Mr Umpleby and 'Uncle Jim' always looked ill, each tinged with yellow, though the one was rather stout and pasty, the other cadaverously thin. I used to wonder whether the heat dried them up! The Umplebys did not have a car but then in the 1930s few of our neighbours did. Mr Umpleby always walked to and from the mill.

On the other side of us were Horace Wright, an auctioneer, and his wife, Nancy. Mr Wright's business lay with agriculture. When we moved to Flanshaw Lane, he had only recently started out on his own after working for the firm of A E Wilby, and a major source of his income was selling livestock at Huddersfield Cattle Market or at the Wakefield Cattle Market in Denby Dale Road which had once been the largest in the north of England but which closed in 1963. He had an office in Cleckheaton. He was a tenant wright and valuer as well as an auctioneer. A bluff figure, always dressed in a suit, with a watch chain across the waistcoat, but often with Wellington boots over his trousers, he would hail us cheerfully as he went out in his car or returned home. Sometimes he would bring us a live wild rabbit. We would try to keep these in a hutch but they never lived. Today we would have recognised that his wife was an agoraphobic. Perhaps she was anorexic as well. She was very tall and extremely thin with a small round head perched on a long neck. She had a tiny button nose that was always red. In the very warmest weather she would venture outside in a long brown coat and a brown velour hat and would walk slowly round the house. She never seemed to go as far as the road or even the gates. We used to wonder what she did all day since she had women who came in to do the cleaning and perhaps also the washing and ironing.

Four pairs of semi-detached houses on the opposite side of Flanshaw Lane had been built by George Crook. They varied from the modest – the two pairs opposite our house – to the magnificent – the pair furthest away from us and nearest to Dewsbury Road. In these two grand houses lived members of the Crook family themselves. The back of their houses overlooked the Westgate Brick Company's quarry which George Crook's family owned and where clay was extracted.

Between the Crooks' houses and the next pair was a footpath which ran across fields along the top side of the quarry. One of my favourite occupations as a child was to stand staring down to watch the trucks of clay being pushed across the quarry floor, then fastened onto a large hook and hauled up the ramp to the brickworks itself.

Between the path and the edge of the quarry were pigeon lofts where men whose names I never knew, and who were probably miners, kept their racing pigeons.

In the pair of stone-faced houses on the eastern side of the footpath lived the Cravens and next to them, when we first moved to Flanshaw Lane, the Tunstalls. Stanley Craven was a director of the engineering firm of Bradley and Craven. Norman Tunstall was the principal of the Technical College. Although we played with the Craven children, especially Robert and Julia, our parents were more friendly with the Tunstalls. I recall our being invited, *en famille*, to a Christmas party at their house and everyone dancing to *Here we come gathering nuts in May*.

Almost opposite us, but set back from the road and at right angles to it, was the beautiful sixteenth-century Flanshaw Hall surrounded by gardens. This was owned by Marjorie Wolstenholme, daughter of

Wakefield Cattle Market. *Wakefield Historical Publications*

Flanshaw Hall. *The author's collection*

a former minister of Zion Congregational Chapel, but it had fallen on hard times and, although Miss Wolstenholme lived in a part of it herself, it was divided into four cottages.

Closer to the road, in the grounds of Flanshaw Hall, was a small terrace of stone-built cottages. The first horror I faced was the death of one of the occupants, Mrs Edith Hesselgrave, whose clothing had been set alight by a chip-pan fire. I heard the thuds and saw the blazing figure as she tried to beat out the flames by throwing herself against a fence.

There was a second auctioneer living at our end of Flanshaw Lane, Ernest Glover. He was a kindly but serious man, thin, rather wizened and stooping when we knew him. Again he had no car and we would see him setting out for town each morning carrying a battered attaché case, walking along the Lane perhaps to catch a bus in Dewsbury Road. He was one of the first of our neighbours to get a television and for some years he would invite my father to watch the *Horse of the Year Show* with him. We did not acquire a television until 1960 when my income as a teacher was sufficient to rent one for the family.

There was, we knew as children, a whiff of scandal about Ernest Glover. His wife Laura had eloped with George Jackson, the manager of Wakefield Building Society which operated from a splendid high-Victorian building in Westgate. The full extent of the scandal became known only in 1976, twenty-seven years after Jackson had retired. On 29 June Lieutenant Colonel Simon Green, chairman of the directors, learned from auditors that some £600,000 was missing from the 130-year old Society's funds. William Robinson, who had been the general manager since Jackson's retirement in 1949, was suspended and subsequently charged with theft and fraud. A Methodist lay preacher, he had over the years set up nineteen bogus accounts and forged title deeds and conveyances, lending the money for these 'mortgages' effectively to himself. In 1978 he was tried at Leeds Crown Court and given a six-year prison sentence. But it emerged that the special green ledgers in which these fictitious accounts were recorded dated back even before Robinson's time and that he had advanced large sums to George Jackson as well as himself. Jackson had, in fact, died in 1970, but without its being discovered, owing the Society £252,000. His will was described as 'complex' but Robinson, who was granted probate, was the sole trustee. Laura Glover was still alive but was then almost ninety and was a geriatric patient at Snapethorpe Hospital. The Society's auditor for many years had been F W T Mills, a one-time mayor of Wakefield. Although he had sold his practice in 1951 to Ernest Corscadden, he continued well into the 1970s to handle the Building Society's accounts. It was only when new auditors, Wheawill and Sudworth, took over that the thefts were exposed. There had been very real fears that, once the crimes were made public, there would be a disastrous run on Society funds but before the scandal was reported in the press arrangements were well in hand for the business to be taken over by the Halifax Building Society and further disaster was averted. Wakefield Building Society, which had been founded in 1846, came to an abrupt end.

Premises built in 1878 for the Wakefield and Barnsley Union Bank which later
housed the ill-fated Wakefield Building Society. *Wakefield Historical Publications*

When I was four, in 1937, King George VI and Queen Elizabeth came to visit Wakefield. The only other formal visit by a reigning monarch had been in 1912 when George V had come with Queen Mary. We were taken to see the royal couple as they passed in an open car through the streets of the town. I have no idea where we stood although I recall being distressed that other people had flags to wave and we did not. The cavalcade entered Wakefield by Doncaster Road and then went on to Wood Street via Kirkgate and the Bull Ring. At the Town Hall they were greeted by a fanfare from the Sheriff's trumpeters and the band of the King's Own Yorkshire Light Infantry played the national anthem. The town's most senior officers were presented to them along with representatives of different churches, trade and commerce. A similar parade of leading figures from the West Riding County Council was brought before them at County Hall. The local paper reported the event as the 'most notable day' in Wakefield's history since 1912 and spoke of the 'impressive manifestations of loyal enthusiasm'. All I remember is that it was very cold.

There had been comparatively few visits by Royalty to Wakefield before 1937 although there were actually two in that year and many more following the accession of the present queen. Queen Victoria never stopped in Wakefield although she did pass through the town by train. In 1858, when she went to Leeds on 7 September to open the new town hall, the efforts of Wakefield townspeople were quite amazing. Local industries gave their employees a holiday. Everywhere within sight of the railway line was hung with flags. A Union Jack was stretched right across Westgate and the prison gatehouse in Love Lane was hung with greenery. A cannon which had been retrieved from the siege of Sebastopol was brought out from Taylor's coach factory in George Street where it had been painted, and was taken to a field close to Ings Road where it was fired at intervals throughout the day. It was said that the noise unnerved the queen.

Apart from watching the trucks at the quarry, how did we spend our days? The area was still quite rural, indeed Leonard Mellor, who was for a time a Wakefield councillor and who had a bungalow a few doors from us, kept goats in the field opposite his house. Flanshaw Library opened there in 1956. We gathered frogspawn, or tadpoles, from the ponds in the fields near the quarry, between Flanshaw Lane and Alverthorpe Road. The Wrights' house had a cellar and I recall one year that our tadpoles developed into tiny frogs and migrated there. More safely, we fished for tiddlers in the beck which ran in those days through agricultural land parallel to Batley Road. Immediately after the war the fields between our part of Flanshaw Lane and the beck were developed by the Corporation as Flanshaw council estate. The first shops to be built by the Corporation after the war, at the end of 1951, were erected there. They were also the first three-storey properties to be built by the local authority and were innovative too in that no timber was used in their construction – they were all steel and reinforced concrete. Within a decade much taller buildings were constructed.

Sometimes skipping was the fashion and we would join the children of Ashleigh Avenue where a rope was stretched across the road and eight or ten of us jumped as one at each end turned it. We chanted rhymes like:

> *I am a girl guide dressed in blue,*
> *These are the things that I can do*
> *Bow to the king, curtsey to the Queen*
> *And turn right round to the washing machine*

At home I spent hours as a child in the 1930s and 40s at our bedroom window doing 'statistics'. This meant noting down every vehicle that passed along Flanshaw Lane. I never retained the columns of figures. But it passed the time. There were horses and carts – sometimes the corporation dust carts, sometimes carts bearing the fruit and vegetables of the greengrocers who sold at the door rather than have a shop. There were two in our area, Blanchard and Towlerton. Mother always bought from Blanchard though the quality was poorer than his rival's. And of course there were cars, vans, lorries and bicycles, and occasional buses. There were no refrigerated vans or articulated lorries then.

Once a month my father visited each of the power stations which supplied the Grid in his section, to 'read the meters'. The task was to check how much electricity had actually been taken into the Grid. I often went with him on these trips. My favourite visit was to Thornhill where the power station lay beside the Calder and Hebble Navigation. Whilst Father was inside the station, I would walk by the lock and talk to the lock-keeper's wife. All power stations were noisy and malodorous places but my least favourite was Barugh where the noise and smell were the worst.

Unity House in 2005. *The author*

Mother liked to shop at the 'Co-op' and regarded the dividend as her own money. Almost all my mother's spending power came from my father. He kept meticulous accounts (I still have his notebooks in which every major item of expenditure was recorded over a period of well over fifty years) and he insisted on checking the housekeeping money every night. From the next bedroom I used to hear him patiently questioning my mother about her day's spending and teasing out the answer to a missing penny or twopence.

We went quite often to the vast premises of the Wakefield Industrial Co-operative Society in Westgate. This had been founded in 1867 when officers at Wakefield Prison realised that the food for its inmates was bought at wholesale prices. They asked the prison accountant whether they could be supplied with provisions at the same rate. He could not help them in his professional capacity but he suggested that a co-operative society might be the answer to their need. The prison governor and its chaplain supported the idea. A public meeting was called and a motion to establish a society for the 'sale of food, clothing, household and other goods' was supported. In 1876 premises for the thriving society were built in Bank Street. In the next few years branches were set up in Kirkgate, Thornes Lane, Belle Vue, Normanton and Featherstone. The Bank Street building expanded into Westgate and Smyth Street with a vast extension in 1901, later to be known as Unity House.

This Co-op building was a wonderful warren of a place. There were individual shops for footwear, groceries, pharmaceuticals and clothing, each of them with a front door on Westgate and a rear door opening onto the broad corridor which ran the length of the building. On the first floor was the vast Unity Hall, available for hire for dances and other activities. The Wakefield Amateur Operatic Society put on its shows there and gradually invested in mobile tiered seating and stage equipment. Up a further flight of stairs were the Minor Hall and other meeting rooms. For a time the Civic Society held its lectures there. Collecting dividend meant going up to the first floor and along a quite narrow, panelled side-corridor to an office where the money was paid out.

The Co-op was taken over by the Barnsley British Co-operative Society in 1962. The new supermarkets killed its business and, with comments from the management about the disloyalty of their customers, it closed in February 1971.

The building was held to be an asset for the community and Wakefield Corporation bought it in 1972 and renamed it Unity House. Among its tenants was the Yorkshire Conservative Newspaper Company with offices for the local *Evening Post* reporters there. The Corporation also bought the Co-operative Society's shop in Westmorland Street. But the District Council decided it could no longer maintain Unity House and it was sold in 1998 to Mark Leatham of Leatham Estates and is leased to Luminar Leisure.

I was six when the Second World War began. We were, I suppose, in a privileged situation as my father's position as the transmission engineer for the National Grid meant that there was no question of his being called up and he had an additional ration of petrol because the car was vital to his work. We were issued with registration (or identity) cards and with gas masks and we carried them with us to school. We also acquired a bucket with sand in it and a stirrup pump in case the house was hit by an incendiary bomb. At school we practised filing into the cellars. At home we had no air raid provision and when the air-raid siren sounded we simply packed together under the dining-room table. There was a public shelter a little further down Flanshaw Lane and we went there once but the assembled company was not appealing and we never went again.

There was food rationing of course from 1940. But my mother kept hens and this meant that we had plenty of eggs and an occasional chicken to roast. What we especially missed were the imported fruits, bananas and oranges. We registered for the rations of bacon, cheese, and butter with Storrow's, a 'corner' shop in the older development a little way down Flanshaw Lane.

A family of refugees from the Channel Islands came to live just across the road from us in 1940 in a part of Flanshaw Hall.

Wakefield escaped very lightly. A bomb on 28 August 1940 exploded in Norton Street on the Elm Tree estate at Belle Vue destroying four houses completely and damaging eleven others. A raid on 16 September destroyed a house in Barnsley Road and left craters in nearby farmland. Another bomb fell in December 1940 in Chantry Road on the Lupset estate. It did not explode but it left a crater some fourteen feet deep. The worst raid was on 14 March 1941 when six houses were demolished in Thornes Road and six people were killed including two young boys.

The former Storrow's shop, Flanshaw Lane, in 2005. *The author*

We went to Sheffield the day after the 1940 blitz there to find my grandfather's church, St James's, demolished by a direct hit and all the windows blown out of his vicarage. The house of a family friend had been completely destroyed but she and her mother had survived.

The war gave Wakefield its largest hospital, Pinderfields. This was opened in 1939 and initially provided accommodation for evacuees from Hull and London before they were dispersed to billets with Wakefield families. In 1940 it became an emergency hospital; the first military casualties arrived on 18 February. Although the war ended in 1945, casualties continued to arrive until the spring of the following year.

Our family doctor was the widowed Mary Purdie. In the days before the National Health Service was established we were 'panel' patients. My father paid a regular sum which then covered our treatment such as it was! Mary Purdie, a tall, slim woman in tweed suits who wore blue-smoked glasses was driven on her home visits by a uniformed chauffeur, Ledgard (never Mr Ledgard). She must have qualified when it was still both unusual and difficult for women to enter the medical profession. She was a formidable woman whose home, surgery and dispensary were in South Parade. Her two sisters lived with her and one acted as her dispenser. I doubt whether she was very good at diagnoses but her style was such that a visit made one feel better. In the early years of the war I developed abscesses in my ears. There were no antibiotics, of course, and the treatment recommended was the continuous use of hot kaolin poultices. Several times a day, Mother would heat a tin of this sticky substance, paste it onto pieces of lint and then clap it against my ears, binding the lint tightly to my head with crepe bandages. The treatment continued for months. I could, of course, hear nothing whilst the poultices were in place. I was stricken like this at the time of another bombing raid and, as we cowered under the table, I imagined bombs dropping all around us and the explosions rumbled in my head. No one thought to explain to me that nothing much at all was happening in reality and I expected the roof to come down on us at any moment.

I was away from school for months at a time with these abscesses. Sometimes the fever was so bad that I became delirious. But much of the time I lay in bed reading.

I have always read a great deal. But for my older sister and I the public library was forbidden territory. My mother feared that the books would carry germs. Instead we had subscriptions to Boots' library on the upper floor of the shop in Kirkgate where the clientele was supposed to be cleaner! Boots closed its libraries in the mid 1960s but we had begun using the public library in Drury Lane long before then.

The war brought tragedy to our neighbours, the Wrights. One of their two sons, Douglas, died when the Cunard liner, *Lancastria*, which was rescuing British troops in the weeks after the Dunkirk evacuation, took a direct hit and sank on 17 June, 1940.

Our parents never spoke to us about physical relationships, pregnancy or childbirth. Whatever I knew of reproduction came from whispered revelations by fellow pupils at school but I did know that mothers-to-be became rather round. In 1944 it seemed to me that my forty-year old mother might well be expecting another baby. She said nothing about this at all. One day, while I was having a bath, she came into the room most unusually in her underwear. The bulge was entirely manifest. 'You must be having a baby,' I burst out. There was a moment's silence and then, 'Well, I have begun to wonder,' she said. She consulted Dr Purdie who was clear that there was no pregnancy. It was simply that Mother, always on the stout side, had entered the menopause. There were no pregnancy tests or scans in the 1940s. But I think that Mother would have been entitled to extra food rations and perhaps to bottles of orange juice or cod-liver oil. After further consultations Dr Purdie referred my mother to a specialist in gynaecology. He took no more than a few seconds to declare that Mother was at least six months pregnant. He could hear the baby's heart beating strongly.

Both Paula and I had been born at home. In the 1930s, when there was much more class-consciousness than is the case today, middle-class women had their babies either at home or in private maternity homes. Wakefield's first municipal maternity hospital, which had been opened in a converted house in Blenheim Road in 1919 was not, it was thought, for the likes of us. But by 1945 all that had changed. In any case, it would have been taking quite a risk for a woman the wrong side of forty to give birth without round the clock professional maternity care. My younger sister, Enid, was born on 11 February, 1945 in the purpose-built Manygates Maternity Hospital which had opened ten years earlier replacing the Blenheim Road one. After Mary Purdie had so let us down, when the National Health Service was founded we left her practice and registered with the partnership of Drs Thomas Walker and Archibald Heron who had surgeries in Southgate and at their homes in Manygates Lane and George-a-Green Road. Dr Keith Souter, who joined the practice in 1979, traced its history. The burgeoning partnership had originated in the 1850s when Henry Horsfall, one of three brothers from Wragby – all doctors – moved his Wakefield surgery from Manor Court Yard to Southgate. The development of the Ridings Shopping Centre led to a move to a site close to Northgate in 1981. The most recent move, to spacious, purpose-built premises in Buxton Place, came in 1999. It is still known as New Southgate Surgery.

We celebrated victory in the war against Germany in May 1945 with a bonfire in the field next to the Cravens' house. Stanley Craven brought a great deal of material to fuel it.

Manygates Maternity Hospital in use in 2005 by Bretton Hall College. *The author*

In the years immediately following the war, Wakefield still seemed a friendly and quite forward-looking place to live. There was a fair amount of community activity. There were the 'holidays at home' weeks in August each year when everybody seemed to flock to the parks. There was a great civic event in 1947 when Field Marshall Viscount Montgomery ('Monty'), the hero of El Alamein, was given the Freedom of the City. Montgomery came to Wakefield on 4 November. He travelled from York in a Rolls Royce but from the city boundary at Stanley he came to the Town Hall in his 'Old Faithful', the staff car that had carried him across the deserts of Tripoli. There was a parade in Wood Street of various battalions of the King's Own

37

New Southgate Surgery, Buxton Place in 2005. *The author*

Drury Lane Library in 2005. *The author*

Light Infantry, the Cadets from Silcoates School and Dewsbury Wheelwright Grammar School, and the Wakefield Sea Cadets as well as other semi-military organizations.

My elder sister, who had always been unhappy there, left school in 1947 and found work as an assistant in the library in Drury Lane. It was the first time any of us had set foot in the place. A modest, single-storey building, it was opened only in 1906 despite the Act of Parliament in 1850 that encouraged local authorities to provide libraries for their townspeople. It soon became almost a second home to me as, with a baby sister and all the infant paraphernalia crowding our house, I chose to go there after school to do my homework.

In 1948 the electricity supply industry was nationalised. My father now worked for the Central Electricity Authority which, in 1957, developed into the Central Electricity Generating Board. The re-organisation meant promotions for my father but more of a desk job, too, first in Leeds and later in Harrogate. However, as a transmission-construction engineer he played a substantial rôle in the development of the great power stations at Ferrybridge and Eggborough. Our world was changing and Wakefield was too.

CHAPTER 2

SCHOOLS

My mother was determined that we should have a good education and, in her view, than meant Wakefield Girls' High School. The school had been opened in 1878 by the Governors of the Wakefield Charities, the body which was responsible for Wakefield's Queen Elizabeth Grammar School, in Wentworth House, a Georgian mansion in Wentworth Street built at the beginning of the nineteenth century for John Pemberton Heywood. The school provided for 'young ladies' aged eight to eighteen, in a period when there was considerable pressure for girls to have similar opportunities for secondary education to boys. There were differences: there was strong opposition to girls taking part in games, and science, too, was considered unsuitable. Girls had the alternative of taking Needlework. However, Hockey was introduced in 1893 and classes in Science commenced in 1894. The Fives Court was built in 1899. A chemistry laboratory was added in 1905. But

Wentworth House in 2005. *The author*

even in 1918, when Norah Mulligan began her thirty-year stint teaching Chemistry, science was regarded 'rather as a handmaid of Mathematics than as a subject in itself' and girls still had the option of taking Needlework instead. The games fields, at a little distance from the school in Richmond Road, were bought in 1909. The First World War led to the school premises becoming a military hospital in 1917 and the school itself became nomadic, meeting in rooms in the Technical College, then in Sunny Lawns, Sandy Walk, at 8 St John's North, and at St John's Institute. In my days there some of the rooms still bore the names of the wards, Wellington and Kitchener, for example. The Jubilee Hall was opened in 1928, marking the school's fiftieth anniversary. Its foundation stone had been laid in 1927 by Princess Mary, the daughter of George V, who, as the Countess of Harewood had become Yorkshire's own member of the royal family.

From 1881 the High School had a preparatory department for both girls and boys aged from five to eight. Paula and I were both enrolled in this preparatory school when we were five. The classes for

The rear of Wentworth House in 2005 with the Jubilee Hall on the left. *The author*

The author, on the left, and her elder sister Paula about to be taken to school by their father in 1938. *The author's collection*

five to eight year olds were in the Willows in Margaret Street presided over by Elsa Engvall who was to serve for thirty-two years before she retired in 1955. A tall, gaunt and grim woman, she should surely never have been allowed near tender infants. There were four classes, Kindergarten, Lower and Upper Transition and School Remove.

I was a forward child. I had taught myself to read by the age of three, largely by puzzling out the characters on cereal packets, and I resented being placed in Kindergarten where the days were mainly spent in play. I was thus soon in Lower Transition under the harsh eye of Grace Waller. Where did the school recruit those stern, grizzled spinsters? I feel sure they were strong believers in original sin. I never recall a smile or a kind word from either Grace Waller or Elsa Engvall. Children were there to learn not to. Not to anything in particular. Just not to. For some reason I was invited once to the Manchester studios of the BBC to take part in a *Children's Hour* broadcast. Miss Engvall was firmly against such a trip. I went, anyway. My younger sister, Enid, followed me into Kindergarten in 1950. Elsa Engvall wanted her removed because she was 'too precocious'. Once, being forced to sit at the lunch table until she

The Willows, Margaret Street in 2005. *The author*

would eat her ill-cooked sago pudding, she coldly refused and ordered the staff to telephone our father.

When I first went to the school, in 1938, it took boarders as it had done since the 1890s. Queen Elizabeth Grammar School, which was founded in the late sixteenth century, had in fact attracted boys from a distance at least as early as the eighteenth century. They, like the first High School boarders, lived in lodgings rather than in premises provided by the school. Boarders in 1938, however, lived in school accommodation in houses in St John's Square where the Governors had taken numbers 3, 5, 6 and 9. Some of the staff, including Elsa Engvall and Grace Waller, lived there too. There Grace Waller had a huge loom on which she wove her own curtains (and perhaps the cloth for her customary tweedy suits). She also kept an allotment on land bordering Margaret Street. Did she detest teaching as much as some of us detested her? If so she had a long period of endurance for she was at the school for twenty-five years.

It was a forbidding atmosphere but in class I thrived. We learnt to do simple sums with the use of 'tens bundles' – little bundles of blue sticks, not much bigger than match sticks. The only class reading book I can remember was *Carrots: Just a little boy* by Mary Molesworth. It had first been published in 1876 but I suppose we read aloud from the edition of 1920. I think the little boy, Carrots, stole a sovereign. Of course I had no idea what a sovereign was and it did not occur to Grace Waller to explain. Questions were not encouraged. It has always seemed to me odd that teachers question children whereas it is the teachers who know the answers.

I did not thrive outside during playtime. I have never been in the least bit athletic so that the climbing frame – or jungle jim as it was called – held unspeakable terrors for me. I was a little happier in the two-person rocking boats and when I acquired a little boy friend, one Leslie Howarth, I could endure playtime if he and I commandeered one.

The threat of war brought a black pupil to the school. Ports such as Liverpool and Bristol had had a small coloured population since the days of the slave trade but in Wakefield we had never seen anyone with a dark skin. Olaremi Salisu came from Nigeria brought back by a Wakefield woman, Mildred Goodall, who was working as a missionary. No doubt feeling that her foreign name was unsuitable, the school insisted that the poor girl be known as Margaret. The outbreak of war prevented Miss Goodall returning to Nigeria with her charge and Olaremi remained at the High School where her guardian's sister, Lucy Goodall, who lived at Panel House in Northgate, taught Art. Olaremi proved an excellent athlete and no bad scholar. She remained at the High School right through to its sixth form and went on to Durham University before returning to her native country. We were always good friends and on her later visits to England she sometimes made contact again.

The headmistress for most of my schooldays was Kathleen Kingswell. She had been appointed, when still Kathleen Maris, in 1933. When she married, in 1940, she was the first married woman on that all-female staff. Her very presence inspired silence and awe. She conducted prayers each morning and as her gowned figure moved down the long corridor towards the Jubilee Hall a great silence fell over the gathered school. The whole of the senior school assembled in the Hall, from the eight year olds upwards, all standing in rows throughout the session. This, with a hymn, prayers and notices, and sometimes a harangue, could last up to thirty minutes. Not surprisingly there were exciting occasions when someone fainted.

In 1941 I moved up to the 'big school' to Form I in the main building, in Wentworth House. Now each subject was taught by a different teacher. For the first three years the curriculum concentrated on English and Arithmetic, History, Geography, Scripture (the focus was solely on the Hebrew and Christian scriptures, of course) and such genteel pursuits as Art, Singing and domestic crafts. We also had periods in the gymnasium and afternoons at the games field.

Needlework and Domestic Science were taught by Miss Muir, a formidable Scots woman who paid no heed to progress: she intended us all to eat and dress well in primitive conditions. It was axiomatic that we would make our own clothes, and without the aid of a sewing machine. We became experts on run-and-fell seams and embroidered button holes. I mastered one very useful skill – the ironing of shirts. (I still do them rather well!) Electric irons were also banned, however. The school's flat irons were heated at an open fire and we tested their warmth by the sound they made when we patted them with wet hands. Miss Muir would never have encouraged us to spit on them!

Cookery lessons were held in an upper-floor room at the back of The Willows, approached by an outdoor staircase, a fire-escape I suppose for the staff who had flats up there. We made buns and cakes in ovens at the side of fires. Miss Muir was a devotee of the stock pot – a large pan which hung over the fire for weeks and months on end into which we were taught to put bones, scraps of bacon, and left over vegetables. Ladles of liquid from the pot, we were told, could be the perennial basis of soups or stews. It is not something I have ever tried at home.

Gymnastics and games held for me the worst terrors the school could offer. In charge – and it often felt as though she was in charge of the school as well – was the doughty Ruth Benson who had come to the High School as Senior Physical Education Mistress in 1933. The woman was, I later realised, an aristocrat to her fingertips. She had a deep but quite musical voice and dark shingled hair and much of the time she wore a green gymslip with its hem well above her knees. Beneath this she wore green knickers. We knew this because she kept her handkerchiefs tucked under the elastic of their legs. It was a strategy she recommended to us. We wore navy-blue gymslips and square-necked white blouses. Our hems had to be four inches above the knee and Miss Benson would make us kneel so that she could measure them exactly.

I did well – often brilliantly – in other subjects but I was hopelessly incompetent in the gym: I never could vault over a 'horse' or leap onto a box, nor could I climb ropes. Once, falling over a 'horse' I broke a finger. I have a permanent reminder in its subsequent crookedness. My school reports for the 1940s include comments from Miss Benson like 'Coral must improve her posture', 'Her head position needs care', 'She must try to develop more spring', 'She must learn to move with grace'.

Some years after I had left school, Miss Benson became a good friend. There was general shock and sadness when she was killed in a road accident on 5 December, 1959. I recall her warning me, when I was planning to ride a motor scooter to work, that vehicles were 'a lethal weapon'. So her bubble car proved. Gates to the school in Margaret Street were erected in her memory and blessed on 6 May, 1963.

Miss Benson taught us to swim – not that I ever progressed beyond a clumsy breast stroke (although I remain brilliant at floating on my

This photograph of High School girls, taken in 1951, shows the traditional uniform of gym-tunic and square-necked blouse. The collared blouses and ties distinguish sixth-form pupils. *The author's collection*

back). We went to Wakefield's old baths in Almshouse Lane. Here the changing cubicles were built around the bath itself. It was a small, and quite intimate place, the bath being only seventy feet long and thirty feet wide and, at its deepest, a mere six and a half feet. It had been built in 1874 by Wakefield Public Baths Association at a time when it was estimated that fewer than twenty per cent of the Wakefield population had access to a bath in any form. Shares were priced at £1 to allow members of the working-class to buy them. It was not a commercial success and was taken over by the local authority in 1884. In February 1977 the building was deemed unsafe and it was closed and demolished.

Although I was terrified of getting out of my depth, I enjoyed the brief sessions we had at Almshouse Lane.

Not So Merry Wakefield

Occasionally my father took us to Wakefield's 'new baths' in Sun Lane. These had been opened in 1938. The pool itself was much larger than the Almshouse Lane one and the changing rooms were separated from it with a foot bath between the two. But it was a noisy place with considerable echoing from the shouts of the swimmers and divers. I was far happier at the old baths. I have never seen the inside of Wakefield's most modern swimming baths at the Lightwaves Centre which was opened in 1989.

We had regular 'medicals' at school in the presence of Miss Benson, with the school doctor, who was also our family doctor, Mary Purdie. Mrs Kingswell had initiated the medical examinations in 1934 and they were held in her office. They focused on our eyesight (mine has always been excellent, I am happy to say), our chests and our feet. I was thought to have a weak chest and this was treated by regular sessions at Clayton Hospital where I donned dark goggles and was exposed to ultra-violet rays. I was also thought to have flat feet and a routine of exercises so drastic was imposed that I have suffered from excessively raised arches ever since.

I saw more of Clayton Hospital in June 1944 when I had my tonsils and adenoids removed. The National Health Service was still some months away and my father could not afford the fees for my staying as an in-patient, so I was operated on at about ten in the

Lightwaves Leisure Centre in 2005. *The author*

morning, lay suffering and spitting blood on a couch in a small white-tiled room until mid afternoon, and was then taken home.

The High School in my day was a Direct Grant school, receiving financial support from central government rather than from the local education authority. Besides taking fee-payers, the school also took girls from the age of eleven who, depending where they lived, had won a County Minor or City Minor scholarship and whose fees were then paid by local authorities. The scholarships were introduced by the West Riding County Council in 1891. When Wakefield became a county borough in 1915, it provided the scholarships for pupils living within its boundaries. Text books for scholarship holders – numbered as a check on their return and often tatty – were provided on loan by the school. I sat for, and passed, the scholarship in 1944. My father had struggled to pay the fees for two of us but at least I now attended school free.

There were some entirely ridiculous rules. I can understand the sense in insisting that girls walked in single file along corridors and that the two staircases in the main building were designated as 'up' or 'down'. But there was the insistence that we never appeared in the streets or on buses in our school uniform unless we wore a hat or beret. Tough in windy weather! But what was the point anyway?

Year by year I progressed steadily, entering the Sixth Form in 1949. Mrs Kingswell retired as headmistress the same year to be succeeded by Margaret Aylesbury Knott.

I sometimes wonder whether I gained much at all from school! My knowledge of geography and history (!) remains woefully weak. I did, however, learn enough French to be able to read romantic novels, and I gained a fair understanding of Latin. The Head of Classics, Vivienne Hughes, came to the school in 1945. She was one of the few truly inspiring teachers that I encountered. She had a wonderfully clear mind, a great sense of humour, and considerable kindliness. She also had a wonderful head of auburn hair which escaped intriguingly from the coil on top of her head. In 1951 she married the Wakefield Diocesan Secretary, Albert Nurse. She volunteered to give me some extra coaching in Latin and I visited the flat where she and Albert first lived at the top of Church House, in South Parade, a number of times. She retired in 1971 after serving as Deputy Headmistress for the last three years of her career. She and Albert lived for some years in Notton before returning to Wakefield to make their home in a flat in Blenheim Road. She did not entirely give up teaching as she led a group for Italian conversation for the University of the Third Age.

The subject that has remained with me with the greatest clarity, however, was Mythology. We did this for just a year in the Lower Fourth Form before embarking on Latin. It was taught by Edith Waters whose husband, Sammy, taught at Queen Elizabeth Grammar School. I loved it and I have never lost an interest in Greek mythology or the ability to recall the names of Greek heroes needed to solve crosswords.

Each year I won a Form Prize, a coveted award which was presented at the annual speech day. During the war years the prize took the form of National Savings stamps rather than a book but my father always converted these to cash for me and ensured that I had a book to treasure as a reward. Over the years I collected most of the 'Swallows and Amazons' books by Arthur Ransome. Speech days were lengthy, extremely formal and daunting occasions when we had to sit still and silent except for the singing of the school song, *Hear the ancient watchword ringing, Each for all and all for God*. Prizewinners attended a practice to ensure that they took their prize and shook hands in a systematic and graceful manner. On the day itself to receive a prize one had to negotiate a substantial platform party of school governors, including those representing the local authority. Sometimes one of them had to make a speech. Their broad accents and dropped aitches seemed deliciously incongruous.

The school had choirs and an orchestra. Although never at all skilled as a violinist and handicapped by my badly-mended finger, I played in the orchestra for some years. The most interesting time was in 1947 when, with the addition of some older and more capable musicians, we formed the orchestra for Wakefield's youth pageant, *The Merrie Citie*, which was staged in the Opera House (as the Theatre Royal was known in those days) in Westgate in April in some of the worst weather of the century. It was an ambitious event. Its aim was to bring Wakefield's burgeoning youth clubs together to celebrate the history of the town in a series of scenes each undertaken by a different club. The pageant was written by Edith Waters, of the Mythology classes, and her husband Samuel. They were a formidable but also adventurous couple. Ronald Chapman, his contemporary on the Grammar School staff, said of Sammy Waters that he had a sarcastic tongue and delighted in being disliked! The overture for the pageant was composed by Kenneth Leighton, then a pupil at the Grammar School who went on to be a distinguished pianist and composer and was appointed as the Reid Professor of Music at Edinburgh University.

Until 1950, the school leaving examinations for secondary school pupils formed the School Certificate, which required a pass in five subjects including English and Mathematics, and the Higher School Certificate. Serious work for the former began for me in 1948. The preceding year was a remarkably relaxed one. At the end of September a farmer's daughter, Claire Falshaw, who had a sister at the school, asked for volunteers to help with the potato harvest. The war had created a severe shortage of farm labour and groups of us were allowed to miss two days of school to join Claire for the task. Nine of us were in the first group. We went by train to Haigh Station – one of the many closed following the Beeching Report of 1963 – and walked from there to the farm. All day we followed the tractor as the earth was turned and the potatoes exposed. There were two prisoners of war who came from the nearby camp at Woolley. It was the first time I had met Germans but they were good natured, hard working men. All that bending, picking, and hauling the baskets of potatoes! After the authorised two days I had had more than enough. However, back at school the following day, I got a message that I was needed again after the weekend. The second team had done only one day but had not worked fast enough and most of them had been 'sacked'. Just to prove my stamina, I cycled to and from the farm for the final two days. I have never had the slightest wish to work on a farm again!

In 1949 I gained eight passes at distinction level in the School Certificate, doing less well only in Latin for which I obtained a credit. External examinations changed when I was in the Sixth Form and in 1951 I took A-levels in English, French and Latin and Scholarship-level papers in English and French.

Senior girls were given the chance of a holiday in Switzerland, staying for ten days or so at the *Hotel Alpenrose* in Wilderswil in the charge of Miss Bosward. The traditional trip, held once every two years, had been abandoned after the 1939 visit because of the war but it was resumed in 1947. In 1949 my father felt he could afford to let me join the group. By this time my elder sister, Paula, had left school and, after some time working miserably (but she was always miserable) in the library in Drury Lane, she had gone as an apprentice to work on a farm in Wales. Her fear of the livestock curtailed her progress but the experience came to a premature end when she became ill. She was brought home with Scarlet Fever. This was a serious illness then. Anyone in Wakefield who contracted it was sent to the isolation hospital at Snapethorpe.

The hospital had been built in 1934 to replace a small municipal fever hospital in Park Lodge Lane dating from 1876. Designed by the city architect, Louis Ives, it had separate blocks for Diphtheria and Tuberculosis as well as a general Fever Ward and could accommodate ninety-seven patients. Fresh air being regarded as an important part of treatment, it had verandahs running the length of each ward. It stood at one of the highest points in Wakefield, 270 feet above sea level. It was entirely financed by a private benefactor, James Benjamin Sykes. Sykes was a self-made man and understood the value of every penny! He had left school at thirteen but with his brother had bought the empty Dudfleet Mill in Horbury and developed a thriving industrial concern. To cut building expenses, Sykes bought the mechanical excavator that had been used to dig the foundations of St George's Church at Lupset. He also bought all the wooden shuttering and other timber that had been required during

The porter's lodge at Snapethorpe Hospital, 1935. *Wakefield MDC Local Studies collection*

the construction of Wakefield's new bridge. This provided the scaffolding for the building work at the hospital.

With Paula in hospital, I was put in quarantine and instead of the longed-for trip to Switzerland, I spent my days walking up to the hospital gates to read the bulletins posted there and to leave notes for Paula. My disappointment at missing the expedition was tempered when my father bought me a new bicycle. Two years later, in 1951, I joined the party going to Wilderswil. I kept the bike, too.

The sixth-form years were demanding. I studied English, French and Latin and was a prefect and the Games Secretary, a role which I loathed and which involved arranging both hockey and tennis matches with other schools. The years were enlivened, however, by the opportunities of the Sixth Form Club, an institution run in my day by Vivienne Nurse and Grammar School History master Ronald Chapman, bringing together the senior boys from QEGS and the High School girls. The club had been started in 1941 by the redoubtable Edith and Samuel Waters to provide some supervised social interchange. Many a future marriage was founded there! The highlights of the club's activities were its dances. My partner at these was a former grammar-school boy, Tom McLean, with whom I sometimes went to the pictures or attended concerts. He was some eight years older than myself and a good deal taller! We cannot have been an elegant couple.

I don't recall the school ever providing any careers advice. The assumption was that girls went into teaching (via university or training college) or into nursing. The annual school magazines gave news of old girls only under one or other of those headings. Occasionally there was mention of someone who had braved the world of medicine. It was clearly not done to become a shop assistant! But no one ever seemed to be expected to go on to the 'masculine' fields of law or accountancy, or into journalism although much later the school produced a clutch of able writers.

I had determined that I would go to Oxford, although I knew precious little about it and the school told me nothing. The Sixth Form mistress was Winifred Bosward, of the Wilderswil excursions, another severe soul who taught French and who gave thirty-seven years of her life to the school. I never recall her smiling. Tall and thin with rather a mauve complexion, she had quite piercing eyes. I recall that she was very discouraging when I proposed to apply for a state

High School prefects, 1951. The author is at the extreme left of the front row.
The author's collection

scholarship. She was an Oxford woman herself and I have never quite understood why.

Having failed to obtain a place at Cambridge, which was no disappointment at all, I left the High School in the summer of 1952 shortly before my nineteenth birthday and took up my place at St Anne's College, Oxford, financed by my state scholarship, later that year.

Long after I left, under the Labour government of 1974, the Direct Grant system was abolished. The local authority scholarships went too. The governors of the High School and Grammar School chose to turn them into independent schools although providing some bursaries for children from poorer homes. They are now somewhat exclusive, still single-sex, establishments. I prefer the state-based comprehensive system and rather relished the fact that, when I was a vice-principal there in the 1980s, Barnsley Sixth Form College attracted a number of High School girls (including the writer, Joanne Harris – she was Joanne Short then) and Grammar School boys.

By the time my son was three, in 1961, keeping him at home was almost impossible. I was away for long hours teaching at the far side of Leeds and, despite domestic help, my mother found it too much to cope with a lively little boy. I could find no crêche and was told that the local authority's day nursery at Burmantofts was not intended for the likes of me. I was advised to place Simon with a Barnardo's home in North Yorkshire. It would have been devastating. But I knew that the private Cliff School in Leeds Road took quite young children. I wrote to its principal and proprietor, Nellie Tattersfield, and asked when she might be able to take Simon. Her letter was almost the first kind gesture I had known since coming back to Wakefield. If I was the woman who had been at the High School and had an illegitimate child, she would take him straight away, she said. It was a lifeline. Better still, the cook arrived at the school very early each morning and Simon could be placed in the care of the cook long before the school day really began.

Mrs Tattersfield had opened Cliff School in 1939 in a house in Margaret Street with three pupils. In 1954 she moved the school to St John's Lodge on the corner of Westfield Road and Leeds Road and it was there that Simon went from 1962 to 1966. A year or two after Simon had started at the school, Mrs Tatt, as she was known, invited me for tea at her home in West Bretton and proposed that I should

The Cliff School in 2005. *The author*

join her staff with the option of taking the school over when she
retired. But by that time I had a lectureship at the City of Leeds
College of Education and was, in any case, ironically and despite Mrs
Tatt's kindness, already a strong supporter of state education. Cliff
School was sold in 1968 to Mr and Mrs Mitchell, the proprietors of
Wakefield Tutorial School and Mrs Tattersfield and her husband
retired to live in the south. She died on 15 January 1980 at the age
of seventy-nine. The school was acquired in October 1987 by
Edward and Kathleen Wallace, both qualified teachers, who had
moved up from London. After tremendous growth within the school
and its companies, Cliff School was sold in December 2004 to the
London-based educational group Alpha Plus. Its head by January
2005 was Mrs A D Gleave.

Cliff School was a happy place although in Simon's day pupils seemed to learn little in the way of the three Rs, and some of the teachers were far from qualified.

From there, when he was eight, Simon progressed to St John's Primary School. This dated back to 1861 when the Church of England was expanding its presence in elementary education. Its first premises were in a converted mill in Wentworth Street. New premises for girls and infants were built in Clarendon Street in 1876. But when Simon went there the school was united in a relatively new building in Belgravia Road. Sited on a former refuse tip, the school was built on a raft and was designed as a single-storey building in order to spread the weight as widely as possible. The school had a close relationship with St John's Church where Simon joined the choir. Simon once said that the school was all 'Hands together and let us pray'. But it provided a solid grounding in basic subjects and, under its head-teacher, John James Watson, was a very happy place.

But some of Simon's happiest school days were at the Cathedral School in Thornes Road. This – although re-founded in 1959 – had a long hinterland going back to 1813 when the Bell School was established just off Wood Street. The school moved to Zetland Street in 1869 and in 1895 it became All Saints National School taking over the old grammar school building in Brook Street. The Cathedral School, which moved into its new buildings in 1960, was Wakefield's first post-war secondary school and, under the headship of Harold Speak, arguably always its best. Harold Speak was a dedicated and

St John's C of E School in 2005. *The author*

inspired head and gathered an excellent team of staff around him. He knew every pupil and many of their parents. He fostered plenty of out-of-school activity including clubs for history (his own favourite subject) and astronomy. While he was there, Simon went on an historical re-enactment exercise at Conisbrough Castle. The children made their own 'armour' and camped at the castle for the weekend. In today's climate of litigation, such ventures would be circumscribed by lengths of red tape.

Education is vulnerable to fashion and to both central and local government decisions. In 1972, the Wakefield Education Committee went in for wholesale reorganisation. The Cathedral School, which had formerly taken pupils up to the age of sixteen, became a middle school and, at fourteen Simon was too old to remain there. Many of his friends were to go on to Thornes House but, because we lived close to Eastmoor estate, the local authority insisted that he must go to Eastmoor City High School. Its reputation at that time was far from reassuring. I was acquainted with Dr Evans, the headmaster of Silcoates, and his wife and they urged that I send Simon there. I had grave misgivings but it seemed the only realistic option. From Anglican schools, Simon went on to non-conformity.

Silcoates originated in 1809 in Silcoates Hall as a proprietory school, the Yorkshire Dissenters' Grammar School. It was refounded in 1831 and in 1832 was named the Northern Congregational School. It provided boarding education in particular for the sons of Congregational ministers and for very many years it had a close association with Zion Chapel in Wakefield.

When Simon went to Silcoates, in 1972, it was very much a second-class grammar school and for boys only. Ambitious and class-conscious parents sent their children there if they failed to obtain a place at Queen Elizabeth Grammar School. The standard of academic education was poor although the school had an excellent tradition at sport. Simon elected to take cross-country running, a pursuit which has given him a stamina which lasted well into his middle age. One of the masters was keen on canoeing and not only taught the boys how to wield their paddles but also oversaw their making their own canoes. I think it was very probably the long hours spent sandpapering the fibre-glass hulls without wearing any industrial mask that landed Simon in Clayton Hospital to have his sinuses drained. But those were the days before litigation and we never inquired into the cause. On one splendid occasion a group of boys were taken with their canoes to West Tanfield, in North Yorkshire, to canoe along the River Ure.

Careers advice at Silcoates in the 1970s was no more advanced than it had been at the High School twenty years earlier. Simon was not academically inclined although he was markedly able in practical skills. Of course the school was quite desperate to keep boys into the sixth form and I was naïve enough to believe their advice. He should, we were told when he was sixteen, find a career in boat-building (it would have suited him admirably) but the first requirement, we were also told, was to continue to A-levels. It did not occur to the masters to tell us that craft apprenticeships were for sixteen-year olds, not for boys of eighteen. I do not think that anyone in Simon's year gained any respectable passes in any A-level subject and he was left, at eighteen, in a period of high unemployment, with no A-levels, only a modest clutch of O-levels and with no more viable qualification than his driving licence.

Woolley School in 1992. *The author's collection*

I became associated briefly with the village school in Woolley in 1992 when it was scheduled for closure and the then vicar of Woolley, Kenneth Pearson, asked me to write its history. There had been provision for education in Woolley from at least 1564. My account was published in 1993 at the time the school actually closed. The school building then became a village hall and community centre. It had been for well over a century a caring local school taking children from Woolley and Notton but falling birth rates, well-to-do parents sending children to private schools, and the need for economies in local-authority education brought it to an end.

CHAPTER 3

TRAUMA

I went up to St Anne's College, Oxford in the autumn of 1952 with a state scholarship. I was not quite 'trailing clouds of glory' but I was certainly successful, respectable and rather admired. I returned to Wakefield in the summer of 1958, pregnant, unmarried and irretrievably alienated from the baby's father. My parents were, of course, devastated but at least they allowed me back home to live – in shame and the focus of much gossip. Attitudes to 'fallen' women were still very harsh at that time. I earned what I could by freelance writing, in particular by a series for the *Yorkshire Post* on some of the new writers carving out fresh fields for fiction – Kingsley Amis, Iris Murdoch, John Wain, and the Yorkshire writer John Braine among them. I managed to interview them all, even staying overnight with the Amises in Swansea, and having dinner tete-a-tete with John Wain at his home in Reading. They were all unfailingly kind. Few Wakefield people were! I also marked O-level Literature scripts for the Oxford Delegacy of Local Examinations, a chore which I continued to undertake until 1979 and which enabled me to buy my own home and ruined every summer.

Wakefield's principal maternity facility was Manygates Hospital (which was to close in 1992). But there was also a maternity ward at the County General Hospital in Park Lodge Lane, which had evolved from the infirmary of the Wakefield Union Workhouse. Of course the days of the workhouse were long gone.

I arranged to go to the County General Hospital for the child's birth. Somehow the favoured Manygates Hospital seemed too respectable. I just wanted somewhere where I could be as anonymous as possible. Perhaps it was a mistake. The birth, on 2 December, was difficult and, when a consultant was called in, he said immediately that I had needed a Caesarian section and that it was by then too late. I was taken to the operating theatre and my son was, happily, safely delivered. The maternity staff assumed, without asking me, that the baby would be put up for adoption and forestalled any breast feeding.

I lay in bed, sick, scared, lonely and depressed, watching proud fathers bring their tributes of roses to the other mothers.

But I was adamant, even in the face of my father's opposition, that I would keep my son. At least I persuaded his father to go with me to register his birth and to give him the acknowledgment of his surname. It was all that we ever received from him.

My mother insisted that after childbirth one had to be 'churched'. It seemed to me a quite horrible superstition and my distaste and embarrassment may have contributed to my increasing distress. But I followed her wishes – I was ready to yield easily over little issues but held firm over the big one – and went to St George's Church, Lupset, for the rather furtive ritual and the sinister words: 'The snares of death compassed me round and the pains of hell gat hold upon me'. Other women might enjoy their babies. I was expected to feel nothing but guilt and shame.

I did not recover from the birth itself or from the wretched experiences in the hospital. And, perhaps sensing my sorry state, the baby never slept for long and spent most of his waking time crying.

St George's Church, Lupset, in 2005. *The author*

And I needed to get work. The doctor prescribed tablets for depression and more tablets to help me sleep. I began to feel dependent on drugs to get me up and more drugs to get me to bed. And, quite simply, I rarely seemed able to think straight.

I had spent two of my college long vacations as a reporter on the staff of the *Yorkshire Post* and had proved rather successful earning a good many by-lines. I had also done some book reviewing for the paper so it was actually easy to persuade the editor, Sir Linton Andrews, to give me a job. I would have to travel to Leeds each day and would be expected to work the 3pm to 10pm shift quite regularly. I had no money for a car and, although the idea terrified me, I thought that the best way to travel would be by a motor scooter. When I tried to ride it, I felt even more odd – like being both drunk and sober at the same time. As my first day at work approached, I became less and less lucid. No one seemed to understand – I was just being 'difficult'. And, of course, as an unmarried mother with a difficult baby, I must have been regarded as nothing but a nuisance. The day before I should have begun at the *Yorkshire Post*, I ran a high temperature and was very sick. It was a relief to think that I might have 'flu.

In the next few days I went downhill very quickly. I had dreadful hallucinations and only brief periods of lucidity. The worst moment, for everyone, was when I walked down the stairs quite naked as someone arrived at the front door. A magistrate was summoned and I was 'sectioned' – committed to Stanley Royd Hospital under a warrant. I was vaguely aware of the ambulance speeding along Eastmoor Road and of being taken into an office for the admissions procedure, but I was beyond answering any questions myself. I went entirely out of my mind. I had puerperal mania.

Stanley Royd Hospital had been built in 1818 as the West Riding Pauper Lunatic Asylum. Besides short-term patients like myself, who were expected to recover, there were numbers of people who had been inmates for much of their lives. There were also some who were in the final stages of senile dementia, lying in beds that seemed to me, in rare moments of consciousness, to be more like coffins. I was in so serious a state that I was isolated and shut in a cell-like room with nothing but a mattress on the floor. If I had wanted to get out, I could not have done. There was no handle on the inside. Every so often the door would be opened and a commode chair pushed in. At

Stanley Royd Hospital in 1964. *The John Goodchild Collection*

other times, I was checked by an eye at the peephole in the door. For the first two weeks I was mostly 'vacant'. When I was in some way more aware, I could not figure out who I was or where I was. I thought that I must be in hell.

I think that I owe regaining my wits to Electro Convulsive Therapy. I do not know how many 'treatments' I had. I was aware of one occasion and of the terrible headache that followed it. Then, and it seemed to be entirely suddenly, I came to my senses. I was completely and utterly rational. I now had a bed in my cell and the shutters were open. I knelt up and looked out of the window. I could see trees and a bus passing in Stanley Road. There was a real, normal, world out there. I wept with joy.

I remained in the hospital for about three months. Although I was, or so it seemed to me, sufficiently recovered, I was kept there to undergo a course of insulin therapy. This was a brutal treatment. It

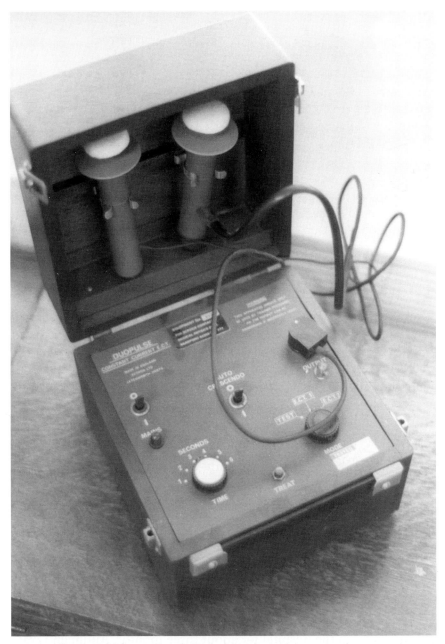

The machine used to administer Electro Convulsive Therapy.

involved being put into a coma, by means of an injection of insulin, every day, early in the morning, and then being brought round by having a sugared solution introduced into one's stomach via a tube taken up one's nose. Once one was fully conscious one was forced to eat a massive breakfast. There was always the risk that one would lapse into a coma again. The small group of patients undergoing this treatment was kept together all day and constantly watched. On the first spring days we were taken for walks in the hospital grounds. One of the nurses pointed to grotesque figures separated from our group by high netting barriers. She told me that they included people who had had puerperal mania like myself in the days when the condition was not understood and no effective treatment was available.

Sometimes we were taken to a dance or to see a film in the hospital theatre – no, not an operating theatre but a real, fully equipped entertainment venue. This was built by those enlightened county magistrates in 1859 for the benefit of both patients and staff.

I do not recall ever attending St Faith's Church which stands inside the hospital railings at the corner of Eastmoor Road and Stanley Road. This, too, was provided by the West Riding Magistrates. The plans were copied from ones prepared by George Gilbert Scott for St James's, Doncaster, and it was consecrated in 1867. In 2005 it stands derelict although Magna Holdings have plans to reinstate it as offices or flats. The original hospital block is, however, a listed building and in 2004–5 it was converted into prestige flats.

Slowly I recovered. Then, of course, I had to find work. There seemed little chance by now of persuading the *Yorkshire Post* that I would prove an asset. And then there was the press strike. We thought that, as television became increasingly important, newspapers might never recover. I would have to look to teaching instead. I had no difficulty in obtaining interviews although I thought it wisest not to seek employment close to home – my situation was too well known and the stigma attached in those days to unmarried mothers was too great. Among places I attended for interview was the Girls' High School in Barnsley. As soon as I explained my situation, the headmistress's attitude changed completely. No job there. But shortly afterwards I was offered a post as a qualified graduate assistant teacher at Roundhay Girls High School in Leeds. I accepted gratefully. And then the blow fell – a letter from the headmistress

The main building of Stanley Royd Hospital in 2005 after conversion into flats. *The author*

expressed her great regret that the offer would have to be withdrawn: there had been a tennis match between pupils from Roundhay and those from the High School in Wakefield, staff had gossiped; whilst she fully understood how disappointed I would be, she feared that her pupils would very soon know too much about the new teacher.

I was devastated. But – and perhaps the months in the mental hospital had contributed to this – I had developed a great deal of resilience. Rather than wither, I simply wrote a very angry letter to the headmistress of the High School, Margaret Knott.

Oddly, as it turned out, the loose-tongued staff had done me a good turn. Within days of my rejection at Roundhay, I was invited to Leeds to meet their Chief Education Officer, George Taylor, and a woman inspector, a Miss Ayres. It was another example of the unmitigated kindness some few people offered me. They apologised for the way I had been treated and said that Leeds owed me a job! They offered me a place immediately on the staff of West Park

County Secondary School. In fact I later realised that the school was in some difficulties and when I began work there, there was still a staff shortage so perhaps George Taylor's offer was not purely philanthropic! I was promoted after a year and given responsibility for the school library. After four years' teaching, I was, it seems, head-hunted for a lectureship at the City of Leeds Training College where I would train other teachers. The six years there, where I was promoted to a senior lectureship after two years, were some of the happiest of my professional life. Briefly, I went on to be principal lecturer in English at Wentworth Castle College of Education, Barnsley, for a further ten years and when that closed in 1978 I became a vice-principal at the new Barnsley Sixth Form College. It was based in the very same premises that had held Barnsley Girls' High School where I had been rejected in 1959.

It must have been hard for my parents to provide a home for their errant daughter and her son. However, I was able to assist fully with all household bills and to provide the family with the luxury – as it still was – of a television. In 1963 I bought my own car, a necessary asset for visits to supervise trainee students on their 'school practice', and during college holidays was able to take my mother on visits to the east coast where my elder sister and her husband lived. These were, perhaps, small compensations. But in July 1966 my rôle changed and I became both nurse and housekeeper. I had been woken one Friday night in July by the noise of someone falling. I found my mother on the floor of the lavatory. Father and I were able to raise her and help her back to bed, but when I went into my parents' bedroom in the morning, I could see from the lop-sided appearance of her face that she had had a stroke. I have often wondered why my father refused to let us call the doctor. It was of no consequence. I ignored him and asked my younger sister, Enid, to go to the neighbours to 'phone the doctor from there. Dr Heron confirmed that Mother had had a stroke and suggested that it would be best if she were nursed at home. It was the college vacation and, since I had studied for a home-nursing qualification at Clayton Hospital, there seemed to be no reason why I should not take charge. Life became an endless cycle of patient-care, child-care, cooking, washing, ironing and cleaning. And by mid-September I was back at work full time as well. We managed. Friends and neighbours looked in on my mother during the day and we also had some domestic help.

Gradually Mother regained her speech and the ability to walk although her right arm always hung limply. She took to the life of an invalid with some fondness, staying in bed with a radio until mid morning and returning for a rest each afternoon. But one of my clearest memories is of ironing sheets until the small hours of the morning, weeping with weariness.

Then, just as it seemed that Mother was recovering well, she became mentally ill. First it was just a matter of compulsive obsessive behaviour – constantly washing her hands, checking endless times that the taps had been turned off. But she grew more and more irrational and was certain that someone was trying to kill her. We could not leave her in the house alone and a stream of neighbours and friends took turns to be with her. Pills were prescribed. The strain was making my father ill, too. I insisted that the doctor called in a consultant and he immediately recommended treatment in a mental hospital. Stanley Royd, where I had been so successfully treated in 1959, was thought not to be good enough for Mother. An amenity bed was found at Scalebor Park Hospital at Menston, and Father and I took her there on 23 March 1967. When we visited her only a few days later she had been transformed. Electro Convulsive Therapy had restored her too to normality. She stayed there for six weeks and we brought her home in May, a new woman. She was fit enough to go away the same month with my father for a few days to Thornton-le-Dale.

My father retired in September 1967. This made life much easier. He could now take over some of the housekeeping. I decided that it was time Simon and I had a little more of a life and began to explore the possibility of buying my own home. Single mothers were not well regarded by banks or building societies when a mortgage was at issue. However, I had begun to make modest investments with Friends Provident and their financial adviser took a kindly interest in my situation. He was, as it happens, a Freemason and perhaps that helped. He found that the Bradford and Bingley Building Society would advance a mortgage and named the price range of property that would be acceptable. I took my time looking at houses – always in the St John's or College Grove area, always quite near my place of birth. I knew what I wanted – a detached property with a garage, central heating, and a spacious living room.

In 1969 I bought my own home at 19 Pinder's Grove, a development that had been built in the earlier 1960s in the grounds of Clarke Hall. I still live there. A number of houses on the Grove had been taken by the Home Office and were let to some of the senior staff at Wakefield prison or at the Staff College in Love Lane. I had been looking for a house for almost two years. I had even once looked at a house at the bottom of Pinder's Grove but been put off by the cramped entrance hall. It was in a very damp November in 1968 that I responded to a small advertisement in the *Wakefield Express* for a detached house for sale not far from the centre of Wakefield in my price range of £5,000 to £5,600. I was disappointed when the voice on the other end of the telephone line gave the address. But there was nothing to be lost in going to look at it so an appointment was made. The moment Lois McKelvie opened the door to me I knew this was the house I wanted to buy. Unlike the one I had seen earlier, it had a nice open entrance area. When she showed me the study and I saw on the shelves so many of the books I had for my own job – works on the English language, volumes of poetry and plays, books of criticism – I was ready to pay the full, and actually rather modest, price. Donald McKelvie had a position similar to my own in the English Department at Scawsby College, Doncaster. He and his wife had fallen in love with a period house at Easingwold and hence the Pinder's Grove home was for sale. We could not move in until 31 March, 1969 but I never had a moment's regret about the choice.

Now Simon and I lived alone in quite roomy surroundings. At last I had my own longed-for study downstairs, still with Donald McKelvie's bookshelves, and Simon had a playroom upstairs as well as his own bedroom. There were other families with children of Simon's age and he quickly made friends. Parents of both sexes now went out to work and in the school (and my college) holidays we kept open house. Frequently I would pile the children into my car and take them into the Dales or to the coast. We also went regularly to the swimming pool in Royston where the neighbours' children all learnt to swim and dive under my very elementary tuition.

The M1 motorway was fully opened between Leeds and London on 18 October, 1968. It had already claimed the lives of three workmen when, on 23 August 1967, a section of roadway being lifted to bridge the River Calder at Durkar, collapsed. My son, Simon, was fascinated by the motorway and, indeed, by other great engineering projects like the Humber Bridge which was opened in 1981 and the M62 which was built between 1970 and 1976. We planned to visit my sister Enid in London the day the M1 motorway was finally opened and waited at the roundabout at the Dewsbury Road intersection for the tape to be cut and the drive to commence.

The new road made trips to London and Oxford remarkably easy. It also provided my route to work when I moved to Wentworth Castle College. But it was to be the site of tragedy for our family.

My sister Enid, her husband Jim, and their seventeen-month old daughter Emma, came to stay with my parents for the Whitsuntide holiday in 1971. Jim hired a car and on Thursday 27 May they proposed an excursion with my parents into Derbyshire. I called in at home in Flanshaw Lane on my way to college that morning. My mother was still in bed and begged me to persuade them to let her stop at home. Was it a premonition? I laughed off her fears and cajoled her. They would have a lovely day, I said. Fatally, she went with them.

At the end of the college day, I collected Simon from the Cathedral School and we came home to Pinder's Grove. We had just finished our evening meal when the telephone rang. Was I Mrs Barron's sister? a voice enquired and repeated more insistently, Was I Mrs Enid Barron's sister? 'This is the accident and emergency department at Clayton Hospital,' the caller said. 'Could you please come?' I demanded to be told what had happened but was simply advised to get there. I would be told then. I knew that something very grave had occurred. Telling Simon that he must come with me at once and that something dreadful had happened, I made for the car. 'There's been an accident, and I think someone has been killed,' I said to Simon. 'But who?' The picnic party had included both my parents, Enid, Jim and the baby Emma. I dreaded what I would find. How many had died? Mentally I went over the possible fatalities and knew that, if either Enid or the baby were dead I could not bear the news. I drove the car flat out along the centre of Eastmoor Road. 'There'll be someone else killed if you don't slow down,' Simon remarked. Parking in the hospital forecourt, we rushed to the accident department. I saw Jim immediately, seated in a chair with Emma on his knee. She was soaked in blood but was otherwise clearly unharmed. That was one anxiety eased. A nurse came forward and took me first to a cubicle where my father lay, conscious but in pain, then to another where Enid was receiving treatment. Then I was taken aside. 'I am afraid that your mother is dead,' I was told. A few moments later a police officer came and took me to the morgue in Brunswick Street to identify her.

The Canning Child wing at Clayton Hospital which was provided in 1932 as a gift from Samuel Canning Child and which housed the accident and emergency department. *The author*

The mother I had seen in bed that morning now lay naked in a mortuary drawer. I was given a plastic sack with her clothing in it, saturated in blood. As they were returning to Wakefield by the motorway, somewhere close to Calder Grove, the car had spun out of control, hit the banking on the central reservation and turned over. Mother, who had a broken back, had died in the ambulance. Back at the hospital I asked for food and a change of clothing for Emma. Father and Enid were wheeled up and down to the X-ray department. Father had broken ribs. Enid had been flung through the windscreen and dragged along the road. Her legs were a mass of lacerations and were full of fragments of broken glass. Father asked me where Mother was. He thought she had been taken to one of the wards. I had to tell him that she had died. 'I thought we would have had a few more years together,' he said pitifully.

I cannot blame Father and Enid for wanting those of us that were left to stay together. They refused to remain in hospital. Somehow I got them all back to Flanshaw Lane. I collected a few things for Simon and myself from Pinder's Grove, and we went back to stay there to care for them.

I have always believed that one of the most important things at times of crisis is to maintain a steady daily routine and to ensure that people have rest, regular warm drinks and nourishing meals. Those, and washing all the soiled clothing, became my priorities. There was the death to register – I took my father to do that – and then I had to attend the opening of the inquest. All that was needed was for me to identify the body I had seen as my mother's. At least I had the short break from college for the Whitsuntide bank holiday and a week's leave because of the bereavement. There was a full, and harrowing, inquest later. Because the car had been hired, there was a major issue of culpability and of an insurance claim. The car firm hired a barrister. We were represented by a Wakefield lawyer, Harry Moxon. The barrister first hoped, I think, that Mother might have been killed by reckless driving. When that proved a non-starter, he wanted a verdict of death from natural causes and tried to make much of the fact that she had had a stroke. The forensic evidence quashed that. He was desperately trying to ensure that no blame fell on the company which had supplied the car. The police evidence was crucial. The tyre had been penetrated by a three-inch nail which, they asserted, could have been picked up only at the garage. The wear on the tyre from the nail head was consistent with the mileage Jim had done since he hired it. The company had, simply, supplied a defective vehicle.

But our lives had been changed for ever.

CHAPTER 4

CHURCHES AND CHAPELS

My mother was the daughter of an Anglican vicar, Dawson Parsons, who, when I was born, was the incumbent of St James's, Sheffield. She was always firmly Church of England and of the 'low' church or evangelical persuasion at that. My father's family were, for the most part, Methodists although he had himself had a brief association in Sheffield with the Plymouth Brethren. Church or chapel-going was central to our childhood although where we actually went varied considerably.

Almost every place of worship we attended has since closed and been demolished. Some of my earliest memories are of going to the 'tin tabernacle', St Mark's Church, in Pinderfields Road. My parents must have gone there when they first came to Wakefield and the link was maintained after we moved to Flanshaw Lane. St Mark's had been opened in 1896 as a mission church for St Andrew's when the surrounding area was developed for housing. It was dedicated by the first bishop of Wakefield, William Walsham How, but even the opening was low key. St Mark's was the simplest of worship spaces, just a corrugated iron hut with, inside, wooden chairs facing a communion table. There was a reading desk but no pulpit. In the middle of the church was an iron stove, with a pipe going up through the roof. It would sometimes glow red hot. The chapel had a small organ in the far north-eastern corner. My father installed an electric blower for this and I sometimes played it for the services. Even in those days, in the 1930s and 40s, the congregation was always very small – sometimes only seven or eight in number. I suppose the services were taken by the vicar of St Andrew's, or the curate when the parish had one, but I recall occasions when no minister arrived and my father provided impromptu leadership.

St Mark's closed in 1975. Two houses stand on the site today. The closure followed the building of St Swithun's on the Eastmoor estate, as a daughter church to St Andrew's in 1959 and the amalgamation of the neighbouring parishes of St Mary and St Andrew in 1966. Both St Mary's and St Andrew's had been carved out of the large parish of Wakefield in 1844 but slum clearance after the second world war had taken away much of the population of St Mary's. The chairs from St Mark's were taken to the Chantry Chapel which had been in St Mary's parish but which, as a result of the amalgamation, lay in the extended parish of St Andrew.

For a time my elder sister and I went to the Sunday School at Dewsbury Road Methodist Chapel which was only a very short distance from our Flanshaw Lane home. This had been built for the Primitive Methodists to serve the vast Lupset housing estate. It was opened on 3 July, 1929. The architects of what was described as 'an excellent example of modern church architecture in its simplest form' (in other words graceless red brick!) were Dinsley and Moss of Chorley in Lancashire. The builders were the ubiquitous local firm of George Crook and Sons. At its opening the chapel had no minister but was in the pastoral care of a lay preacher, W H Lawrence. His daughters, Edith and Constance, taught in the Sunday School and when an extension was built in 1963 it was Edith who performed the opening ceremony. Dewsbury Road chapel was next to the Roman Catholic school of the English Martyrs. Until their church was built in 1956, the services were held in the school. Ecumenical relations were unheard of in 1930s and 1940s Wakefield (The Churches

The Church of the English Martyrs, Dewsbury Road, in 2005. *The author*

Together movement was not founded until 1990) and the clearest recollection I have of the Sunday School there was of being harangued about the evil of the Catholics.

It was many years before I set foot inside a Roman Catholic church but, as a child, I found Catholicism rather glamorous. To celebrate Corpus Christi, the English Martyrs had a splendid procession which wound up Flanshaw Lane and onward to the Dewsbury Road premises. I loved the swinging of the censer, the colourful vestments, and the bearing aloft of a statue.

Just occasionally we went to Wesley Hall, another Methodist Chapel which lay at the junction of Thornes Road and Horbury Road and was opened on 20 June, 1936. The chapel itself always intrigued me as it was built very much like a cinema with a rake and tip-up seats. At the back was a projection box. Many years later, when I was writing a series of newspaper articles about local picture houses, I realised that Wesley Hall had been one of a number of Methodist chapels built in the form of cinemas as it was felt that members of the working-class would be more familiar with that type

West Wakefield Methodist Church, Thornes Road, in 2005. *The author*

of building and therefore more likely to venture in. At this time J Arthur Rank, an ardent Methodist as well as a cinema pioneer, contributed substantial funds to Methodism for new buildings. Some of the money came to Wakefield.

Wakefield has seen very few new places of worship in the past seventy years. However, the new West Wakefield Methodist Church, opened on the Wesley Hall site in September 2003, replaced both this and the Dewsbury Road chapel. By then Wesleyans and Primitive Methodists had long overcome their differences, brought about by a union in 1933. In addition to the West Wakefield Methodist Church there have been a new Baptist Chapel at Belle Isle and the Roman Catholic Church of St Peter and St Paul lying just off Asdale Road close to Kettlethorpe.

Planning consent for Wakefield's first mosque was granted in 1974. It was a conversion of St Michael's Infant School in Grange Street. At the time there were some 200 Muslim families, living primarily in the Doncaster Road and Agbrigg Road area. Wakefield's splendid first purpose-built mosque, which is also an advice centre and a centre for Islamic education, was completed in 1995.

My mother's search for a spiritual home among the 'low' Anglican churches in Wakefield took us for a time to St Mary's in Charles Street. This too has long gone. St Mary's had been built in 1854 ten years after the area close to Kirkgate Station was separated from the large parish of Wakefield to form a new ecclesiastical district. It was a simple and cheap Victorian Gothic structure. In the days when we

Wakefield's first mosque in 2005. *The author*

St Mary's Church in the 1940s, taken from the passageway from Kirkgate to the railway station. *The John Goodchild Collection*

went there it was heavily blackened by soot. The vicarage, up a few steps in the same yard as the church, was equally black. The Sunday School teaching at St Mary's was as intolerant as that at the Methodist chapel only this time it was the Jews who were anathema. We knew nothing about the Holocaust in the early 1940s but surely Hitler's ravings should have been enough to earn the sympathy of Christian people. Far from it. We were expected regularly to contribute to the funds to support missionary work converting the hapless Jews to Christianity.

Christ Church shortly before its demolition. *The John Goodchild Collection*

It may have been a change of vicar or it may have been the grubby state we came home in, that led Mother to try out Christ Church instead. It, too, has long gone. It was on Thornes Lane. It was built, no doubt, as the low-church alternative to St James's, Thornes. The Anglo-Catholic, or Oxford, Movement of the 1830s and 1840s had its effects in Wakefield as elsewhere. Whilst the Anglo-Catholics reintroduced much of the ritual of the Roman Catholic church, the low churches remained firmly Protestant. Rival individuals or groups sought to purchase the advowsons (the gift of the living) of churches so that they could introduce clergy of their own persuasion, or, indeed, to build new churches. Christ Church was another cheap

Victorian Gothic building financed by Mrs Disney Robinson and opened in 1876. It closed in 1955 and was demolished in 1958 and the parish was amalgamated with St James's at Thornes.

At the High School I became friendly with Penelope Myers, the daughter of the vicar of Hopton. Penelope was, I think, a lonely girl. She had a very long bus journey to and from school and, if there were other children of her age in the village, she was isolated from them by her position as the vicar's daughter and by her parents' choice of school. Her mother, Beryl, tried to remedy this by inviting one or another of us from the High School to spend a weekend at Hopton. Having 'tried out' several other girls, she invited me. It became a regular arrangement. I loved it. I loved the large Victorian vicarage which stood next to the church and has since, sadly, been demolished and replaced by a much smaller house. I had always shared a bedroom at Flanshaw Lane with one or other of my sisters. At Hopton I had a vast room to myself. I loved the vicar's book-lined, shabby study where we sometimes had tea. I could think of little in life that I wanted more than a study very like it. I was very happy with the church services, too. Harold Myers, the vicar, (later to become Canon Myers) was inclined to be 'high', so that for the first time I actually experienced the swinging of incense, genuflection before the crucifix on the altar, and ornate vestments. In due course, Canon Myers decided I should be confirmed and I attended the preparatory classes at Hopton as well as continuing to go there most weekends. Curiously, although Penelope was sent as a boarder to Queen Ethelburga's at Harrogate, I still went to Hopton to stay there alone. The weekends provided a great time for doing masses of homework and for recreational reading too. Detective novels by Michael Innes were among the vicar's favourites. It was Harold Myers more than anyone else who encouraged me to think of going to Oxford.

Some time in the 1950s both my parents transferred their allegiance to St George's Church on Broadway, Lupset which had been built to serve the Lupset council estate and had opened in 1936. This was suitably 'low'. No vestments, no incense, no crucifixes and little concern for celebrating saints' days. For Mother, much of Sunday morning was taken up by cooking the most important meal of the week, Sunday lunch. But she loved to precede all the preparation by attending the Communion service at Lupset at 8am. I often went with her, walking up through the Lupset estate. In due course my father became one of the church wardens. One of his self-appointed tasks was to cut the grass and he would regularly load his battery-driven mower into the car and spend an afternoon in the church grounds.

In the 1970s I became disenchanted with the established church, whether high or low. A coldly rational part of me found its doctrines quite impossible to accept. Then, whilst I had dearly loved his predecessor, Bishop Ramsbotham, I could not stand Eric Treacy (the so-called 'Railway' bishop), perhaps because he was scathing, or perhaps just patronising, about unmarried mothers. Whilst Simon was at St John's School it was prudent to attend services at St John's Church from time to time and when he was at Silcoates I sometimes went to the school chapel which was, of course, Congregationalist. But on the whole I had little time for Sunday worship anywhere.

Then came European Architectural Heritage Year (1975) and my responsibilities included writing about interesting buildings. John Goodchild, a member of the Wakefield Heritage Committee,

Westgate Chapel in 2001. *The author*

suggested Westgate Chapel as a candidate for an article. I had not then even heard of Unitarianism and, like most Wakefield people, was scarcely aware of the eighteenth century brick building next to Westgate Station. John lent me quantities of his research notes but I always liked not only to visit the places I wrote about but also to talk to people connected with them. I arranged to meet the minister, Reverend Ernest Baker. He was a small, very quiet man but there was about him a flavour of spirituality which I had known in Canon Myers and Bishop Ramsbotham but in few other clergy. Posing many questions, I asked him what his congregation believed. His answer amazed and, when I had completely absorbed it, delighted me. 'I don't know,' he said, 'I have only been their minister for six months.'

This was my introduction to the most liberal branch of non-conformity, a movement with no dogma or doctrine and with no test of membership other than a desire to join the congregation. I sampled a service and very soon became a regular attender. Services were not, in their form, greatly different from those I had experienced in other places of worship. There were hymns – many of them ones I had known since my childhood – and readings and prayers. But the readings were rarely from the Bible. And the sermons were really interesting. Often – and this is just as true today as it was in the 1970s – they were about contemporary social and ethical issues but given a Unitarian perspective.

The key tenets of Unitarianism are freedom, reason and tolerance. Whilst the Movement has its roots in Christianity, Unitarians accept that other religions and their prophetic books are just as valid as the Bible. Moreover Unitarians are ready to weigh the insights into the human condition and its sense of the divine that may be provided by literature or, indeed, science. Darwin Day, the birthday of the proponent of the great theory of evolution, has been marked with a service at the chapel. Unitarians also mark Holocaust Day, World Aids Day and International Women's Day. Unitarians accepted women ministers ninety years before the Church of England did.

I became a member of Ernest Baker's congregation and the chapel has had a central place in my life ever since.

Opened in 1752, the building in Westgate replaced an earlier chapel at the junction of Alverthorpe Road and Westgate Common which had been prone to flooding. Catacombs – brick burial chambers in a vaulted

The catacombs beneath Westgate Chapel. *The John Goodchild Collection*

cellar – were designed as part of the new chapel. Interment ceased there in the 1850s with the opening of Wakefield's municipal cemetery in Doncaster Road, although an exemption was made when Daniel Gaskell, Wakefield's first member of Parliament in 1832, was entombed in 1875. The catacombs became something of a tourist attraction and have been opened many times, in particular at the Heritage Open Day weekends organised by the Civic Trust each September.

When I joined it, the chapel trustees owned the Orangery in Back Lane. This had been built as a hothouse for the Georgian home which stands in Westgate at the approach to the station. Quite when the Orangery was built is uncertain but it may have been there by 1790. The intrusion of the railway viaduct across Westgate and alongside the grounds of the Orangery brought gracious living in the area to an end. After a rather chequered period as botanical gardens, the Orangery was bought and given to the chapel in 1850 by Daniel Gaskell to provide rooms for a Sunday School and other educational activities. It was connected to the chapel premises by a

The Orangery in Back Lane in 2005. *The author*

brick tunnel, which is still there, under Back Lane. A house at the gates of the Orangery provided a home for the chapel's caretakers. A part of the Orangery grounds was used for burials. The trustees let the premises to private schools. The Wakefield-born novelist George Gissing had his early education there in a school run by Reverend Joseph Harrison. For many years until 1957 the Orangery housed the Collegiate School, the junior branch of Wakefield Academy.

When I first attended Westgate Chapel, the Orangery was regularly used for whist drives and a dance group. It was also let to Wakefield Art Club. We had the chapel's annual meetings there, meetings of the Yorkshire Unitarian Union, and social events including splendid dinners. My son's wedding reception was held there too. However, it became increasingly difficult to maintain it – and to find a suitable caretaker, as it happens – and in 1991 the trustees sold it to Ploughland Estates. In 1996 it was acquired by Public Arts, a charity which was founded in 1986 to promote art in public places. There is, in 2005, a scheme to build a highly innovative tree-top extension designed by Will Alsop.

The demolition of Brunswick Chapel. *The author*

It was not just the places of worship we attended that have gone. In 1998, for example, Brunswick Chapel on Saville Street, built in 1876, was demolished to make way for houses. Wakefield's foremost Methodist Chapel, West Parade, lying just off George Street, closed in 1963 and was demolished. The Anglican Holy Trinity, on George Street, closed in the 1950s and was demolished in 1957. St Catherine's on Doncaster Road has had a happier fate; it was destroyed by fire in 1993 but has been replaced by a fine new church which serves also as a community centre Ebenezer Primitive Methodist Chapel, built in Market Street in 1838, closed in the 1950s, and in 2005 is the subject of plans for its demolition and high-rise flats in its place.

Zion Congregational Church in George Street closed in July 2002. In my student days, I had occasionally attended services there simply because I had become friendly with some Congregationalists at Oxford. It had a splendid interior and, perhaps because of its strong associations then with Silcoates School, had a sizeable number at its services. In 1978, as its fortunes deteriorated, a false ceiling was put in, below the gallery, to save heating costs but entirely ruining the look of the interior. Dwindling numbers towards the end of the twentieth century meant that, even with that economy, the trustees could not maintain it. The building was sold to developers and its conversion to form flats was begun in 2004.

Wakefield had become a cathedral city in 1888 when the diocese of Wakefield was created from a part of the diocese of Ripon. Wakefield's ancient parish church became the cathedral. In my younger days, there was rarely any occasion to go there; the cathedral and its services would not have been to my mother's 'low church' taste. When the vicar of Hopton, Harold Myers, was made a canon, I used to go to the services when he preached in the Cathedral. Otherwise any association I had with the place before 2000 came from the coffee mornings which the Civic Society held on its terrace in the 1970s. But a connection was made for me when the Chantry chapel on Wakefield Bridge was taken into the Cathedral parish at the Millennium. The Dean and Chapter then became responsible for the running of the little bridge chapel and the Dean joined the management committee of the Friends of the Chantry Chapel. The Friends held fund-raising coffee mornings in the Cathedral's Treacy Hall which had been built to commemorate Bishop Eric Treacy in 1982. On occasions I began to attend special events at the Cathedral. There was an evening of music on 2 October 2004 to mark the seventy-fifth anniversary of the birth of Kenneth Leighton, the composer. The Dean, George Nairn-Briggs, and Chapter were anxious to make the cathedral more visitor-friendly and, among other strategies, devised a Soundwalk – an audio tour of the building – which was launched in February 2005. I went to the launch.

Early in 2005 I received a remarkable telephone call from the Dean. It was to ask if I would care to be amongst those who received the Royal Maundy from the Queen when she visited Wakefield in March. This was in recognition, I believe, of my work as chair of the Friends of the Chantry but I was pleased that the Dean described me on the nomination form as a 'central Wakefield Unitarian'. The Maundy is distributed by the reigning monarch annually on the Thursday before Easter, Maundy Thursday. Queen Elizabeth II has chosen to visit different cathedrals for the ceremony rather than have it always in Westminster Abbey. And so it was that on 24 March I went to the Cathedral, with my son, who is a nurse at Pinderfields Hospital, as my 'helper' to be given the two Maundy purses, one red and one white, by Her Majesty. The white purse contained 1p, 2p, 3p and 4p coins to the value of 79p, the Queen being in her 79th year.

The author and her son at the lunch which followed the distribution of the Royal Maundy on 24 March 2005. *The author's collection*

The white purse held a £5 coin commemorating the Battle of Trafalgar and a 50p piece. The High Almoner, who handed the purses to the Queen was the Very Reverend Nigel McCullough, the Bishop of Manchester but who had formerly been the Bishop of Wakefield. The machinery used by the Royal Mint to produce the coins was made by the Wakefield firm of Joseph Rhodes.

Although the 158 'recipients', as they were called, came from right across the Wakefield diocese, I found other Wakefield people whom I knew. There was Vivienne Nurse who had taught me Latin at the High School, and two other members of the Civic Society Executive Committee – Julia Gilbey and Jean Rhodes. A near neighbour from Pinder's Grove, Josephine Fox, who has been a sister at Pinderfields Hospital was there too. Walter Harrison, who had been the member of Parliament for Wakefield from 1954 to 1987 and who had become a Privy Councillor in 1977, sat immediately behind me at the end of a pew in the north aisle of the Cathedral. As she walked from one recipient to another, the Queen recognised Walter and stopped to exchange a few words with him. After the service both recipients and their 'helpers' were entertained at a substantial lunch at the *Cedar Court Hotel* with the Deputy Mayor, Councillor David Hopkins, and the Bishop of Pontefract. The Queen had lunch at the Town Hall.

I had known some unhappy times but this was rather a splendid day!

CHAPTER 5

INSTITUTIONS AND SOCIETIES

I joined Wakefield Young Farmers' Club when I was eleven, perhaps at its first meeting on 29 March, 1945. My elder sister, Paula, wanted to work on a farm and I tagged along with her. It proved to be a foolish dream on her part but I became a party to it. The club was founded at that heady time when the war was drawing to a close and thoughts were turning to a better future. It seems to have been prompted by one George Ingham and Douglas Hyslop, the latter of Park Lodge Farm, who became its first secretary. The first chairman was a corduroy Adonis, David Wilby. I made my own friends among the younger members, Leighton Smith from Hemsworth who went out to Australia as a teenager under the 'big brother' scheme, and became an authority on grapes and wine, Michael Sturgeon from Paleside Farm at Ossett, and David Parkin from Alverthorpe whose ambition was to be a farmer and who had two rabbits.

The club was for anyone aged ten to twenty-five who was interested in agriculture (or who tagged along, I suppose!). There was an advisory committee of more mature people, including Frank Barker of Bretton and Herbert Greenwood of Chapelthorpe who were both farmers, and Harry Wilson who was an organiser for the National Federation of Young Farmers' Clubs.

In the summer months we met at local farms to judge stock, see demonstrations of tractors or combine harvesters, or just to walk the farm and learn from its owner, tenant or steward about his herds or crops. There were more farms in the vicinity of Wakefield in those days. We went to the farm attached to the Asylum (Stanley Royd as it later became), to Mr Rowbottom's farm at Woolley to admire his Hereford bull, and to the 500-acre home farm at Nostell Priory where the bailiff, a Mr Joule, showed us round. We practised judging cattle at Sowood Farm at Ossett. We also went to Richard Barr's riding stables at Sandal Grange. Some members played a part in the

The Wakefield Young Farmers' Club float at the 1946 Wakefield Agricultural Show. *The author's collection*

Wakefield Agricultural Show which was held in Thornes Park each August from 1946.

The show began as a part of Wakefield's 'Holidays at Home' programme and was held in Thornes Park with further events in the Clarence Park arena. There was a fairground and Punch and Judy show in the arena as well as the Wakefield Flower and Vegetable Show. There were also sports, for both children and adults. The week included a swimming gala at Sun Lane baths.

Exhibitors came to the agricultural show from as far away as Skipton, York, Doncaster and Sheffield. But local farmers took some, at least, of the prizes. The Young Farmers took part in stock-judging competitions, selecting the best dairy cow in milk, and the best beef cattle. I became quite efficient at sizing up bullocks' rumps.

In the winter the Young Farmers held meetings every week in the hall at Clarendon Street School, just off Pinderfields Road. This had been built in 1893 as an annexe to St John's School and catered for infants and older girls. We had talks ('Manure and Manuring', 'Technical Developments in Agriculture', 'What is a Balanced Ration?') or saw Ministry of Information films.

There were weekends away, with young farmers from other districts. I remember once staying at a school in Bingley and going to a grass-research centre to learn about turf for golf-courses and grass for grazing.

There were socials, too, at Clarendon Street and an occasional dance in the Embassy Ballroom. Ballroom dancing had been a popular leisure activity in Wakefield for decades. For many years dances were held in the Assembly Rooms at the corner of George Street and West Parade. These premises had once been the venue for the social activities associated with Holy Trinity Church but had been bought by Ernest Matthewman in 1920. Matthewman also bought the seven-bedroom Holy Trinity Vicarage next door. Later it became the Ace Club and Oasis restaurant.

From its opening on 7 November, 1936, the Embassy in Southgate was the most popular venue for dancing although the Unity Hall in the Wakefield Industrial Co-operative Society building in Westgate ran it a close second. Both halls could be booked for private dances but the Embassy was open six days a week for public events too. Some dances were held in the Music Saloon in Wood Street, formerly the Mechanics' Institute and now Wakefield City Museum. The popularity of television's *Come Dancing* ensured that ballroom dancing continued to be a significant recreation into the 1970s. Mecca opened the Locarno Ballroom in Southgate in November 1959. The name was changed to Tiffany's in October 1970 and by then it was targeting an older age group. It closed only in 1980 when the premises were scheduled for demolition to make way for the Ridings shopping centre. Ballroom dancing nationally was given a fresh spur by the BBC's *Strictly Come Dancing* series in 2004.

The Young Farmers must have taken some part in the Great Yorkshire Show which was held in Wakefield for the third, and last, time in July 1949. The other occasions were in 1846 and 1870. The showground was at Lupset on a site just west of Lupset Hall, with its entrance opposite the junction of Horbury Road and Broadway. Some fifty-four acres were taken up by the showground itself with a further fifty acres or so for parking. The show lasted for three days although the preparations required many weeks. The King's Troop of Royal Horse Artillery were billeted at the Drill Hall in Wakefield for the duration of the show and were provided with a meal each evening by members of the Women's Voluntary Service. On the second day of the show the then Princess Elizabeth and the Duke of Edinburgh came to see it. They went first to County Hall where the princess invested the chairman of the County Council with a new chain and badge. After going on to the Town Hall the royal couple travelled in an open-topped Daimler to the showground. Places were allocated along the route to each of Wakefield's schools. At the show itself, the princess and duke saw a parade of the Badsworth Hounds – hunting was entirely acceptable then – before touring the pens and stalls.

I am not sure how I came to be elected as the secretary of the Young Farmers' Club at the annual meeting in 1946. It was not an experience I can take any pride in! Events were difficult to arrange

The group of Wakefield Young Farmers setting off for Belle Vue Zoo in 1947. *The author's collection*

and I was far from efficient, usually badgering some local farmer about ten days beforehand, to allow us to see round his farm, and publicising the event with an advertisement in the *Wakefield Express*. I also arranged some trips though they had little to do with agriculture, about which, in any case, I knew almost nothing. We had an outing to Scarborough in 1947 which, because of the war, was a novelty. And there was a memorable trip to Belle Vue Zoo near Manchester when only twelve people turned up for the specially-hired coach and it rained all day. But, although I managed to find it interesting enough, the Young Farmers were my sister's people, not mine. My scene is words rather than crops and animals. The club is no longer in existence.

My next venture was to join the Wakefield branch of the Association of Yorkshire Bookmen – far more to my taste. This was founded on 25 October, 1946 with the headmaster of the Grammar School, Wilfred A Grace as its chairman and the city librarian, Robert Sayell as the secretary. It met in the Junior Library on Drury Lane. Its secretary from 1950 for four years, after Sayell had gone to be chief librarian in Watford, was the new city librarian, A J Griffiths, and the chair was taken then by a grammar school English master, W H Teasdale. It was still in existence in 1968. But Wakefield is not a place of high culture and, inevitably, the Bookmen died out. Its members were not themselves writers, nor were they especially discerning literary critics. There were monthly talks but they were mostly by middle-brow writers like the Yorkshire novelist Phyllis Bentley.

Much later I had contact with Barnsley Literary Society which was founded in 1976 but which came to an end in 2004 when it proved impossible to find anyone to take over the task of booking visiting speakers. I was myself engaged for its final talk and spoke about Art and Poverty in the work and life of George Gissing. Many voluntary groups face the same problem today of an ageing membership and a shortage of officers.

In my late twenties, with a young son and a full-time teaching post, there was little question of my having any social life. The swinging sixties passed me by. It was my younger sister's boyfriend, Robin Bellfield, who eventually pointed out that I needed another dimension – and invited me to go with him to a meeting of Wakefield Civic Society! The Society had been formed in 1964 at a time when many of Wakefield's old – often medieval – buildings had been, or were still being lost to redevelopment. The *George Hotel*, on the corner of Southgate and Kirkgate, was at one time 'the most noted commercial hotel in the West Riding'. It had thirty-six bedrooms. In the latter part of the nineteenth century it had been owned by Benjamin Sherwood, the proprietor of Wakefield Theatre Royal and Opera House, and visiting actors stayed there. It closed on 8 August, 1955 and was demolished to make way for the redevelopment of Upper Kirkgate. Three days earlier the *Manor House Hotel* was also demolished. Just three years after the Civic Society had been founded, the *Strafford Arms Hotel,* which stood on the northern side of the Bull Ring at its junction with Northgate, was pulled down. Initially the local authority had refused permission for the demolition on the grounds that Wakefield could not afford to lose the residential accommodation. However the owners, then Bass, Mitchell and Buller, successfully argued at a public inquiry that it was outmoded and obsolescent – none of the bedrooms was en suite – and that it had grossly inadequate car parking; moreover the recently built *Metropolitan Hotel* in Queen Street had never been full since its opening. Clearly, if one took the evidence at face value, the facilities of the *Strafford Arms* were no longer needed. It closed on 31 January

The Bull Ring with the *Strafford Arms* on the right. *Wakefield Historical Publications*

The west terrace, St John's Square, in 2005. The houses threatened with demolition in 1964 are on the left. *The author*

1967. It had been a regular meeting place for a number of Wakefield organisations including the Rotary Club, the Soroptimists and the Historical Society. The Wakefield historian John William Walker noted that Charles Dickens had stayed there, no doubt when he came to Wakefield to entertain with his readings in the Corn Exchange. It was a fine building and made a splendid contribution to the streetscape but it was not to be saved.

Very possibly, without the pressure exerted by the Civic Society, Wakefield's fine late eighteenth-century development, St John's Square, would have been ruined too. By 1964 St John's House, which formed the end of the west terrace, was derelict. Windows were smashed and vandals had begun to trash the inside. Developers applied for planning permission to demolish it and build flats. The Civic Society was prominent among bodies opposing the scheme which would have completely destroyed the Georgian composition. Happily the application was refused and the property was bought by

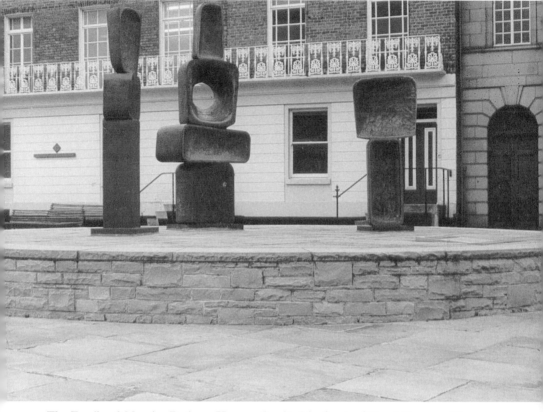

The Family of Man by Barbara Hepworth, sited in front of Bond Terrace. *The author*

the Governors of the Wakefield Charities and was opened on 11 January, 1967 as the junior department of Wakefield Girls' High School. In 1975 the Society had the reward of seeing the Square designated by the Department of the Environment as an area of outstanding architectural interest. In 1977 the Society masterminded a scheme for the reinstatement of the facades of the houses in the Square, overseeing repairs to steps, balconies, railings and windows and reintroducing glazing bars where these had been removed. The properties were repointed and an overall decoration scheme was carried out.

In 1966 the Society made its first awards for new buildings, reinstatement schemes, and landscaping. The refurbishment of

The computer building, County Hall, Wood Street in 2005. *The author*

terrace houses in Rishworth Street and the laying out of a piazza in front of them gained a plaque. Later, in 1977, Barbara Hepworth's composition, *Family of Man,* was sited here. Commendations went to the new fire station in Brunswick Street, the redecoration of the frontages of the terrace in St John's North, landscaping round the new County library headquarters in Balne Lane, the *Metropolitan Hotel* (later to become the *Swallow* and later still the *Chasley*), tree-planting at Newton Green, Leeds Road, and a footbridge off Barnsley Road at Pledwick. Quite unbelievably the Society gave an award in 1970 to the hideous computer building erected at the northern end of County Hall!

The Society's first practical project was carried out in 1966. This involved opening out the 'Cathedral Triangle', a small area of land lying between the backs of shops in Northgate and Westmorland Street and the passageway that runs beside the Cathedral railings. It was a modest scheme but a model of collaboration between the Society, local commercial concerns, and public bodies. Labour for the heavy work was provided by inmates from Wakefield Prison; a commemorative stone was worked by students in the masonry department at what was then Wakefield Technical College; Beverley's Brewery provided a seat.

One of the most ambitious projects the Society has ever undertaken was the laying out of Chantry Walk, an area alongside the River Calder running from Wakefield Bridge towards Fall Ing Lock. The land was given to the Society by Messrs Arnold G Wilson who then owned the adjoining property. It was graded, levelled and seeded, trees were planted and benches and litter bins were put in place. Financial help came from British Jeffrey Diamond, Crystal Spring, and the Wakefield Ladies Circle. The deeds were handed over to Wakefield Corporation, which was expected to undertake all further maintenance, on 8 May 1971. The area has long been neglected. It is overgrown and litter-strewn and graffiti deface the sides of the small stone bridge at the entrance to the site.

Many of the trees which stand in 2005 in the city centre and its suburbs are the result of the Civic Society's 'Trees for Wakefield' campaign which was prompted by the designation of 1973 as National Tree Year. 'Plant a tree in '73' was the slogan. Trees were planted on the south side of Dewsbury Road, beside the river along Thornes Lane Wharf, at Ings Road, Doncaster Road, George Street, Lower Kirkgate, Manygates Lane, Newton Bar, Queen Elizabeth Road, and Wood Street.

The reinstatement of the George and Crown Yard, running off Silver Street, came in 1984. This was masterminded by the Society and included the resurfacing of the footway with stone setts. Many years later the local authority followed on by undertaking a degree of reinstatement of Bank Street and Albion Court and by exposing or replacing setts in Crown Court.

In 1986 the Society oversaw the restoration of Lady Bolles's water tower at Heath. This is both a landmark and a rare example of the domestic engineering that provided an early water supply directly to a house, in this instance Heath Hall.

Much of what the Civic Society achieved was prompted – and often largely organised – by one man, Ray Perraudin, who was one of its founder members and its first president. A Cambridge graduate,

The water tower at Heath in 2005. *The author*

Ray came to Wakefield in 1957 as an assistant education officer for the West Riding County Council after working with the British Control Mission as a university education officer in Germany immediately after the war and gaining his spurs in county administration with the Dorset and Wiltshire Councils. He was tireless, focused and dedicated. He saw how Wakefield could be improved as no one else has done in my experience.

Soon after my joining it, I became the Civic Society's press officer. I still hold the position forty years later. It was my first chance to return to my early love of hack writing. I became the editor of its

Newsletter in 1973 and was the president from 1977 to 1979, relinquishing the post when I became a vice-principal of the short-lived Barnsley Sixth Form College.

The Society initiated a 'blue plaques' scheme in 1994 to mark its thirtieth anniversary and the first ten plaques were provided in 1995. A further dozen plaques were added in 2000 to mark the millennium. One, sited on a house in Manor Haigh Road on the Lupset estate, marks the boyhood home of David Storey 'rugby footballer, novelist and playwright, much of whose work reflects his years in Wakefield'. David, the son of a coal miner, obtained a city minor scholarship to take him from Snapethorpe School to Queen Elizabeth Grammar School in 1944. I scarcely knew him then although he took part in the activities of the sixth-form club as I did. In 1956 he married a High School girl, Barbara Hamilton, whose father was headmaster of Hemsworth Grammar School. After studying art – and at the same time playing professional rugby for Leeds – he wrote his first successful novel, *This Sporting Life*. Published in 1960, it came at a time when gritty northern, and working-class novels, and 'angry young men' were in vogue and was hugely successful. It was made into a film in 1963, shot in part at the Wakefield Trinity ground at Belle Vue. David turned to play-writing in the 1960s and for a time his plays were a success at London's Royal Court Theatre. As with his novels, the plays draw on personal experience. *The Contractor* is in part about putting up a marquee – it fills the stage – and reflects David's experience when he took a holiday job in the late 1940s with Wakefield tent-hire firm, Andrassey's. *The Contractor* was revived by the Oxford Stage Company in 2002 and came to Wakefield's Theatre Royal that summer.

David and I began to correspond after the plaque on his home was erected. Our occasional letters focus on our recollections of Wakefield and our – very different – books.

Joining the Wakefield District Committee for European Architectural Heritage Year was the start of my involvement in writing local history.

The heritage year was 1975. It was a project masterminded by the Council of Europe. The then-new Wakefield Metropolitan District Council set up a committee in 1974 to plan ahead. Its Chief Architect, Ted Cathery, who was as it happens a leading member of

Heath Hall in 2005. *The author*

the Civic Society, became the chairman. Its membership included councillors, local government officers and representatives of the various Civic and Historical Societies to be found across the district including Ackworth, Castleford, Hemsworth, Horbury, Knottingley, Normanton, Ossett and Pontefract.

It seems that at the first meeting, the need for a press officer was brought up. Someone from Wakefield Civic Society suggested me. And so it was that, with some trepidation, I took my place at the end of a very long table, notebook in hand. The committee met in the basement of Heath Hall, home of the redoubtable Mary Oddie and her husband, Muir. The Oddies had rescued Heath Hall from near dereliction and made it a family home, drawing on the expertise of the architect Francis Johnson. Mary gained a high reputation as a conservationist. At my first meeting, plans for marking Architectural Heritage Year were discussed. Someone said that there must be features in the local press about buildings of interest in the area. Someone else asked how this might be achieved. 'That's what the press officer is for,' was the firm answer. I was too shocked and intimidated to say anything.

It is said that when one is really frightened one's hair stands on end. I woke, still horrified, in the middle of that night and the hairs on my arms really were raised.

But the task had to be done. The first thing was to approach Eddie Walker, the news editor at the *Wakefield Express* offices. At least he knew my name from the reports I had been sending in for the Civic Society. I called to see him and told him that we wanted a regular feature which I would write. He shook his head. He did not think that the public would be very interested in articles on places like the Cathedral or Sandal Castle. 'I won't write about them,' I said rashly. 'I shall write about buildings people don't usually notice. I know I can make it interesting,' I added. Eddie was a kind man. He smiled indulgently and said, 'Well, let us have one or two pieces and if we ever have any space we might put them in.'

Among the members of the Heritage Committee was John Goodchild, already eminent as a local historian and at that time still the Curator of Cusworth Hall museum, Doncaster. He offered to help with background information on local buildings. And so I made a start. John had been collecting books and documents since his early teens and had given numerous talks, led many walks, and written quantities of original and scholarly articles on local and regional history. Later he became the Principal Local Studies Officer and Archivist for the new Wakefield Council. He was awarded an honorary degree for 'academic and scholarly distinction' by the Open University in 1984. After his retirement in 1994 he founded his own local history study centre in a large room which he rented in the basement of Drury Lane Library. He continued (and continues in 2005) to amass material – artefacts, deeds, maps, account books, minute books, diaries, letters, and much more – that throws light on the history of the central West Riding. The publications, talks and walks continue too. John's dedication to

John Goodchild at work in the John Goodchild Centre in 2004. *The author*

collecting remains hugely impressive. Everywhere, from derelict buildings, to second-hand bookshops, to car-boot sales, is scoured for relevant items. I well remember a walk when he saw a neglected minute book, almost wholly covered by the mud of a recently bulldozed former colliery site, to be retrieved, carefully cleaned and repaired, and analysed, and when, on the route of a long-disused nineteenth century colliery railway, he found a piece of rail, again later to be displayed at his centre.

John's help was invaluable. He provided me with his research notes on a range of buildings. I visited the places I wrote about and talked to their owners or people associated with them. The first pieces I wrote were on Silcoates House, then the headmaster's home at Silcoates School, and the seventeenth century school house at Heath. They were published immediately and Eddie Walker telephoned me to ask for more.

I tried not simply to write about the buildings in terms of their age

John Goodchild (in the trilby) pointing out features of a quarry at Newmillerdam in 1996. *The author's collection*

and style but rather to explain them, looking at the historical context which led to their being built in the first place and the social change that had affected them subsequently. In the case of almshouses, for example, I would try to find out something about their founders, the nature of the trust deed and how it reflected the attitudes of the time, and the impact a radically changed economy had on them later. I considered, too, the problems of retaining historical buildings when their original purpose had gone and discussed why it might be important to keep them. Some of my articles were mini polemics!

The series ran weekly throughout 1975 and 1976. It was hugely popular. People cut the pieces out and pasted them into scrapbooks or stored them in cabinet drawers. In March 1975 an editorial in the

Not So Merry Wakefield

Wakefield Express noted that 'Not for a long time has a series attracted as much interest among the public as this one, so excellently researched and written by a member of the committee'. Other local historians came forward with research notes or ready-made articles and features soon appeared in the *Hemsworth Express,* the *Ossett Observer* and the *Pontefract and Castleford Express*. John Goodchild was always the mainstay, however. I was by then the head of the English Department at Wentworth Castle College, Barnsley. During college terms, the pressure to produce the weekly columns was intense. I usually got up about 4am on the day the copy was due and dropped the completed article into the offices of the *Wakefield Express* on my way to work. Sometimes I would drive over to Cusworth at the end of the college day to confer with John about further topics. Sometimes I would simply drive around the district looking at its buildings and identifying ones I thought might prove interesting. I became quite bold at knocking on doors and asking the occupants if I could write about their homes. Initially, illustrative photographs were either taken by William Perraudin, son of the first president of the Civic Society, or drawn from archive material in John Goodchild's collection. Later my son, Simon, took on the rôle of photographer.

One of the earliest features in the *Ossett Observer* was on Goring House which was the home then of writer Stan Barstow and his wife Connie. They had lived there since 1961. The house had originated as part of an ambitious scheme in the nineteenth century to make use of the springs there and to turn Ossett into a spa. Stan had enjoyed a major success with *A Kind of Loving*, published in 1960 and later turned into a film. By this time he had three other novels to his credit as well as short stories. He was a local lad who had at one time worked in the drawing office at Charles Roberts' engineering firm.

Despite Eddie's concerns about boring readers with an account of the Cathedral, we did include some churches and chapels – but always the less well-known ones – but my intention was to look at the district's heritage as a whole and that meant anything from its almshouses, banks, colliery villages and co-operative society premises to its parks, schools and warehouses.

The newspaper articles were the major element of the Heritage Year celebrations. However Wakefield's Civic and Historical Societies marked the year with a joint meeting in January 1975 when Keith

Wark, then Adviser in the Humanities with Calderdale Council, gave a talk about Wentworth Castle, Stainborough. He pointed out that, if historic buildings are to be listed for preservation, they need to be selected with a careful and critical eye with some thought for a viable future use.

For a few months, it was a time of optimism for those of us concerned about Wakefield. At the same time as the Heritage Year activity was growing, Wakefield's Planning Department set about designating conservation areas for the City, the first of them in Upper Westgate and Wood Street.

The Wakefield Committee also produced trails. These were devised by other members of the committee and were published in a cheap-and-cheerful typewritten and duplicated format. They focused on Ackworth, the area around Clarke Hall, the canals at Wakefield, Heath, Horbury, the town centres of Hemsworth, Knottingley, Normanton and Ossett, and Woolley. Produced in batches of 200, more than 2,500 copies had been sold by January 1976.

Another concern of the Heritage Committee was to identify buildings which were thought to be worthy of listing by the Department of the Environment. John Goodchild compiled an extensive catalogue including many industrial buildings such as Adingford Mill at Horbury and Flanshaw Mill. The Midland Railway viaducts at Calder Grove and Horbury Bridge, which dated from the early twentieth century, were included. The list was forwarded to Wakefield District Council and became the start of the planning department's register of buildings of local interest. This never provided any statutory protection for them, however.

Eventually it was suggested that the newspaper articles should be published in book form. The first volume of *Wakefield District Heritage* came out in the summer of 1976 in an edition of 2,000 copies. It was launched at a ceremony in the Town Hall. It was so popular that it was reprinted the same year and again in 1978. The second volume came out in 1979. The popularity of the two books has never waned. Copies are regularly stolen from public libraries and from time to time the local authority creates a modest print-run to replace them. Second-hand copies are swiftly bought when they are put on sale in Rickaro's bookshop in Horbury.

As Heritage Year came to an end, the committee was reluctant to disband. It reformed in January 1976 under the title Architectural

The Midland Railway Viaduct at Calder Grove in 2005. *The author*

Heritage: Wakefield District Group. Perhaps its most useful achievement was the publication of John Goodchild's study, *Pope and Pearson and Silkstone Buildings* (1977) which focused on the West Riding Colliery and its community at Lower Altofts. Some of us wanted the group to serve as a pressure group to persuade the local authority to take more care of its heritage. This rôle seemed briefly to have become unnecessary when, in November 1976, the local authority set up its own Conservation Advisory Committee with Councillor Tom Dando as its chairman and with representatives from parish councils and amenity groups. But already it seemed that the councillors had begun to lose interest in the buildings which contributed to the City's character. Already in Heritage Year itself the authority had approved the demolition of yet another significant building in Westgate, the *Cornhill Hotel*, which had been built in 1804–5 as the parsonage for Westgate Chapel. The Committee, later named the Conservation Executive Group, did some good work. It recommended sites for Conservation Area status, invited the Department of the Environment to consider further buildings for listing, gave modest grants for work on listed buildings, invited amenity societies to investigate the state of various listed structures in their areas, and asked the Chief Planning Officer to look at other listed buildings. But it lasted only a short while and was then abandoned.

The launch of the second volume of *Wakefield District Heritage* in 1979. Pictured, left to right, are David Chappell, Ted Cathery, the author, Councillor Colin Croxall and Simon Jenkins. *The author's collection*

Wakefield Historical Society was founded in 1924 at a meeting in the Town Hall. The moving spirit behind this was probably Henry Charlesworth Haldane who lived at Clarke Hall and it was, at its inception, something of an establishment affair. The Mayor of Wakefield, Councillor J W Smith, took the chair at the inaugural meeting and was on the first committee. George Newell was appointed as the first secretary. The great Wakefield historian, J W Walker, was invited to become the first president. The first committee meeting took place in the Mechanics' Institute in January 1925 when the annual subscription was set at five shillings. The first lecture took place in March 1926 in the Paxton Room at the *Woolpacks Hotel* when long-standing Paxtonian C W Carr gave a verbal 'ramble round historic Wakefield'. The first of the summer excursions were to Heath and Kirkthorpe and to York.

For the first three decades of its existence the society did little but provide talks – on very traditional topics – and excursions for its members to very obvious places. Few of its members undertook any research and perhaps it was little more than a social club. But in the late 1950s and early 1960s it became significantly more active. This may well have been due to the influence of John Goodchild and Richard Knowles as well as to its president of the time, Captain Wilfred Craven. It began to publish a journal of research by its members to mark its fiftieth anniversary in 1974. Much more ambitiously, it decided that there should be a full excavation of Sandal Castle. The castle, the principal fortification in the Manor of Wakefield, had been founded, it is thought about 1106, by William de Warenne, second Earl of Surrey and one of the most important Norman barons, who had been given the Manor by Henry I. It would have been a simple earth and timber affair. The following century saw its gradual replacement with stone buildings. It passed, with the Manor, into Royal hands when the eighth earl's widow conveyed it to Edward III. It had been garrisoned in the Wars of the Roses when, in 1460, Richard, Duke of York was besieged by the Lancastrians and the great Battle of Wakefield, in which the Duke was killed, was fought. When Richard III became Lord of the Manor, a new tower was added to the keep. In the latter part of the sixteenth century, the Manor was granted to Edward Carey. In the Civil War it was garrisoned by its then owner, Thomas Beaumont, on behalf of the king. It was again besieged and after the surrender to Parliamentary supporters, it was stripped of its defences. Its active life ended in 1646. For two centuries the site was owned by members of the Pilkington family but in 1954 it was purchased by Wakefield Corporation.

Captain Craven was the first to promote the idea of an excavation but it so happened that the Cathedral School headmaster, Harold Speak, who was also a member of the Society and a keen historian, had been co-opted onto Wakefield Corporation's Library, Art Gallery and Museum Committee. He was thus strategically placed to take up the idea of the excavation with the local authority, the owners of the Castle site. The new chairman of the Committee, Councillor Jack Deen, greeted the project with enthusiasm. However, the Castle is a scheduled ancient monument and no excavation could take place without the agreement of the Ministry of Building and Works. It was prepared to authorise a dig only if it were under the supervision of a qualified archaeologist. A report in the *Guardian* newspaper brought an offer from Phil Mayes, who had just been appointed as Lecturer in Archaeology in the Extra-Mural Department at Leeds University. In 1964 the work began as a joint undertaking between the Historical Society, Leeds University, and Wakefield Corporation. Captain Craven chaired the Joint Excavation Committee. Mayes was able to bring a team of trained supervisors drawn from his extra-mural students. It was one of those few times when Wakefield has seen a truly co-operative and long-term community effort. Captain Craven, who lived not far from the castle, in Manygates Lane, was Managing Director of Bradley and Craven, the engineering firm based in Dewsbury Road, which made machinery for brick-making. He was also, as it happens, a Rotarian and a Freemason, belonging to Linnecar Lodge. He died in 1967 long before the excavation was completed.

The dig took place each year in the summer months. Parties of school children were brought in, organized by Harold Speak. When Phil Mayes was working in the West Indies from 1969 to 1971 Lawrence Butler from Leeds University took the direction over.

Henry Clarkson's *Memories of Merry Wakefield* was published by subscription in 1887. A reprint followed in 1889. A copy of this reprint came to Wakefield Library in 1960 as the result of a bequest by Gladys Taverner Clarke. She was the daughter of Henry Clarke, surgeon at Wakefield prison from 1876 to 1908. The volume left to Wakefield Corporation had been his. Clarke was an artist and the book had been richly illustrated by him with almost a hundred drawings, executed in the 1890s, of Wakefield scenes. The collection of drawings was published by Wakefield Historical Society in 1977 as its journal for that year. It was a commercial success. I joined the Society at about this time and some years later I became its president.

John Goodchild and Richard Knowles, who had prompted the publication, believed that the Society should publish more books but other council members, and the then president, Eric Raper, were reluctant. So John and Richard decided to set up their own publishing group. They invited Heather Lawrence and me to join them in the venture. A request to Wakefield District Council for some financial support led to a donation of £600 on condition that the council was represented on the managing body. And so Wakefield Historical Publications was born with the Chief Librarian, Joe Fieweles, and the Chief Inspector of Schools joining us. I became the chairman and publicity officer and Heather served as the business manager. I had known Heather, then Heather Kilburn, the daughter of auctioneer and estate agent John Kilburn, in our early years at the High School. She was a founder member of the West Yorkshire Antique Collectors' Society. In 1974 her major work, *Yorkshire Pots and Potteries*, had been published. She was also an authority on early maps. None of this prevented her from doing the mundane work associated with publishing, from dealing with the authors and printers to making up orders for books and taking the packages to the post office.

Heather died suddenly in 1984 leaving WHP with a gaping hole. Heather had seen to book production as well as sales. These tasks became mine. They still are!

WHP's first book was researched and written by John Goodchild. *Coal Kings of Yorkshire* focused on members of the Charlesworth and Fenton families and their colliery empires. To our delight, it was serialised in the Sheffield newspaper. It was the first of a number of John's books on the coal industry. Over the years we published *Caphouse Colliery and the Denby Grange Collieries, Coals from Barnsley, Coals from Sharlston, Mine and Men* (about Lofthouse Colliery), *Before the National Coal Mining Museum* (again about Caphouse Colliery) and *Wakefield's First Railway and its Collieries* (about the colliery at Low Laithes). The opening of the museum at Caphouse Colliery, later to become the National Museum of Coalmining, in 1988 provided us with a useful outlet.

Our most ambitious – and most arduous and challenging – venture was to mastermind the financing, assembly and publication of the 372-page report of the excavations at Sandal Castle. We took on Durham graduate Shirley Johnson as its editor. Friction and frustration characterised the enterprise but in 1983, with a substantial input from Wakefield's Keeper of Archaeology, Pam Judkins, the report was published. Magnus Magnusson came to Wakefield City Museum to launch it.

The Victorian novelist George Gissing was born in Wakefield in 1857. His father had a chemist's shop in Westgate and the family

The premises occupied in the mid nineteenth century by George Gissing's family. The Oxfam shop had been Thomas Gissing's chemist's shop. The house extends up Thompson's Yard. *The Gissing Trust*

lived in the property adjoining it in Thompson's Yard. His books provide some of the most telling insights into the social, moral and intellectual pressures of his day. Wakefield has never done much to honour either Gissing or its other eminent literary sons and daughters although a road on the Lupset Estate was named after him and a plaque was eventually erected on the wall of the shop. Gissing was far better known in France, Italy and Japan, and from 1965 Gissing scholars contributed to a newsletter which was edited by a

French professor, Pierre Coustillas. By 1978 it had 250 subscribers. But in 1978 a scheme was devised to establish a centre in commemoration of Gissing in the Thompson's Yard house. The Georgian building, which lies in the Upper Westgate Conservation Area, had just been listed by the Department of the Environment and was in the ownership of Wakefield Metropolitan District Council. But it was empty and had been vandalised. The northernmost part of the house was badly damaged by fire.

A Trust was established with representatives of the Civic and Historical Societies and of the Gissing Newsletter. From its inception, I was one of the Civic Society representatives. Its first chairman was Ray Perraudin, one of the founder members and first president of the Civic Society. The patrons of the Trust included Sir John Betjeman, David Storey, and two other nationally acclaimed authors Gillian Tindall and Angus Wilson. In accepting the invitation to become a patron, Sir John wrote, 'Wakefield is full of good, unassuming buildings of which Gissing's chemist's shop is a good example. Thank you for saving it and the Wakefield mayor and local authority for retaining the character of the town'. It was a somewhat naïve tribute!

An appeal was launched for £50,000 to establish the Centre (it was an ambitious sum and we never reached it). The leading figure in the movement to commemorate Gissing was Clifford Brook, a one-time Mathematics master at Queen Elizabeth Grammar School and later a lecturer at the City of Sheffield College of Education. He became the Trust's first secretary. I was (inevitably, I suppose) appointed as its press officer. Despite protests from the Trust, Wakefield Council authorised the demolition of a part of the house in 1979. However, two years later it was very faithfully replicated. The first real achievement of the Gissing project was Clifford Brook's. He had spent many years building up a picture of Gissing's early life in Wakefield, his schooling at Joseph Harrison's academy and his father's association with the Mechanics Institution which had its premises in what is now the City Museum in Wood Street. He wrote a book on *George Gissing's Wakefield* tracing the associations of the family with Wakefield and the places in Wakefield which featured in his novel *A Life's Morning*. In 1880 Gissing's widowed mother and her two daughters had lived in Stoneleigh Terrace. Gissing's sisters had run a small school from 1898, first in a house in Wentworth

Terrace and later at their home in Sandy Walk. These places and others were noted in a Trail which forms part of Clifford's book. It was published by Wakefield Historical Publications in 1980.

The same year the Trust mounted its first exhibition, in the Library Headquarters in Balne Lane, as part of the Wakefield Festival. The following year the Trust held a major symposium at Bretton Hall. Working with design staff at the local authority's Planning Department, we devised a pictorial trail in the form of a poster which folded down conveniently as a pocket guide. We also commissioned a model of the premises, including both the house and the shop, from Joan Woodward, an expert in creating detailed scale models. This is now one of the exhibits at the Centre. In his remarkable collection, John Goodchild had an inventory of the property made at the time of Gissing's father's death in 1870 so that it was possible to identify the use of every room.

Establishing the Centre took some years. Money did not come pouring in! The Trust recognised that it would never be possible to

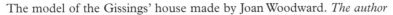

The model of the Gissings' house made by Joan Woodward. *The author*

lease and maintain the whole house. In the later 1980s the local authority leased the whole building to the National Westminster Bank but with the proviso that a small suite of rooms on the first floor of the house should be sublet to the Trust. The bank was immensely helpful. Not only does it still supply the Centre with its heating and lighting, it also financed the carpeting and decoration of the rooms. The scheme for this was put together by Terry Hodgkinson, then managing director of Lemmeleg and much later the chairman of Yorkshire Forward, and myself.

The Centre was formally opened on 5 May, 1990. The aim was to provide somewhere where people could learn more about Gissing but also where Wakefield's literary heritage more generally could be commemorated. From time to time there have been exhibitions there focusing on the work of David Storey, David Mercer, Sabine Baring-Gould Constance Heward and Noel Gay. John Godber, the Upton-born playwright, co-operated especially generously with exhibition material when his achievement was marked at the Centre in 2003.

Recognising that there was little room for exhibits in so small a space, the Trustees decided that video film might be a useful way of adding to visitors' interest. We were able to harness the skills of members of the Wakefield Cine Club and films were taken of George Gissing's Wakefield and of Clifford Brook discussing *A Life's Morning.*

In 2003 The Trust marked the centenary of Gissing's death by publishing a new edition of his 'Wakefield' novel, *A Life's Morning.*

My work for European Architectural Heritage Year meant that I became quite well known at the *Wakefield Express.* One day in 1980 Richard Taylor, who was then the editor of the *Express,* telephoned to ask whether I could write about the history of Wakefield's cinemas. He had seen a series in one of the Norfolk newspapers about cinemas in Norwich and thought that we could do something similar here.

Of course I jumped at the chance – and then had another night where my hairs stood on end. How should I start? Most of Wakefield's picture houses had closed in the 1960s but at least some of them remained standing on the ground. The Playhouse, originally the Picture House, in Westgate could be dated immediately by its foundation stone. Following the 1909 Cinema Act, all buildings where films were to be shown commercially had to be licensed. A useful way to trace the opening dates of the others was by looking at

The Playhouse Cinema, Westgate, in 2005, converted into a nightclub. *The author*

the records of the County Council General Purposes Committee and, from 1915 onwards when it gained County Borough status, the records of Wakefield Corporation Watch Committee. I also did a lot of talking to people, older folk especially, asking them where they had gone to see films and what they remembered of local cinemas. I was puzzled when some told me that they had gone to the Tivoli. The Tivoli? I had never heard of it and it was certainly no longer there. It was, people said, opposite the Cathedral in Upper Kirkgate. Combing issues of the *Wakefield Express* from the 1910s, I found occasional advertisements for this Tivoli, although of course they were not accompanied by a map! Then there was a stroke of luck: the Planning Department was clearing a lot of old files. Some were plans for cinemas and theatres. These they passed on to Wakefield City Museum and the Keeper of Archaeology, Pam Judkins, rang to tell me that one was of the Tivoli. It had been a conversion of assembly rooms in Stockdale Yard. Some time earlier the same premises had provided one of Wakefield's cocoa and coffee taverns.

So the history of local picture houses emerged. In the very early years films were shown at the People's Empire in Teall Street as part of a variety programme. From its opening in 1904, they formed part of the programme at another variety theatre, the Hippodrome, which was also in Teall Street. And programmes of films were presented by itinerant showmen from at least 1902 onwards in the halls at the Corn Exchange and Unity House. Following the 1909 Act, the saloon of the Corn Exchange was converted to become Wakefield's first permanent cinema, the Electric. The elusive Tivoli arrived in 1912. The first purpose-built cinema, and always one of the classiest, was the Picture House in Westgate which opened on 22 December, 1913. A year later came the Carlton in Grove Road and Belle Vue Palace on Doncaster Road. After the hiatus caused by the First World War, another suburban cinema, the Coliseum, was opened in 1920 on Stanley Road. Stanley Picture House was built in 1920 too. The Empire Theatre in Kirkgate became a cinema in 1921. Wakefield's last cinemas, the Regal in Kirkgate and the Savoy at Lupset, were opened a few weeks apart in December 1935 and January 1936.

My researches brought me into contact with people who had worked in the cinema industry or, in the case of Joan Howe at

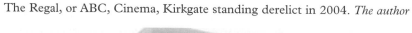

The Regal, or ABC, Cinema, Kirkgate standing derelict in 2004. *The author*

The demolition of the Savoy Cinema at Lupset. *The author*

Stanley, actually owned one of the cinemas. Personal recollections can provide so much more than documentary evidence alone. I learnt from Joe Haigh, most of whose life had been spent in the cinema industry, about how the Gaumont Picture Corporation ran the Empire and the Carlton in tandem and how they hired only one newsreel each week to serve the two cinemas; the re-wind boy would run from one place of entertainment to the other, carrying the film in its can.

The Playhouse in Westgate had been built by Sydney Tolfree who had come to Wakefield originally to run the Hippodrome, a music-hall in Teall Street. His son, Alfred, usually known as Taffy, had come into the business in the 1920s. The Playhouse had been sold in 1956 to Essoldo, the company that already owned the nearby Theatre Royal. I rather wanted to talk to Taffy, but there was the problem of

119

how to find him. I calculated that, with the sort of money he would have received from selling the Playhouse, he would have retired somewhere nice. And Tolfree was not a very common name. So I slowly went through all the telephone directories for seaside resorts in England and Wales, ringing up any Tolfrees I came across, although without tracing Taffy. It was only when I tried the Isle of Man, rather as a last resort, that I found him. He and his wife, Barbara, were living near Douglas. They were delightful people. They promptly invited me to visit them and Taffy met my flight, from Manchester. During the course of an afternoon's gossip, I learnt how the Tolfrees had bought the vast Corn Exchange, that stood at the top of Westgate between Market Street and Queen Street so that they could run the Grand Electric in harness with the Playhouse. In order to obtain the popular new feature films, exhibitors had to take run-of-the mill westerns in the same package. The Grand Electric would do for showing these. It became known popularly as the ranch house.

The great manor of Wakefield, granted to William de Warenne in the early years of the twelfth century, stretched from Normanton in the east to Todmorden in the west and included not only Wakefield itself but Brighouse and Halifax. Its courts dealt broadly speaking with three things – the transfer of property held by copyhold, the payment of debts, and misdemeanours which were not serious enough to go before the justices of the peace. The first two matters were dealt with by the courts baron and the last by the courts leet. The courts were peripatetic and might be held in Wakefield, Brighouse, Halifax or Kirkburton where the church was used for the meetings. Records of the transactions of the courts were kept on rolls of parchment and, later, on paper. These records, which exist in an almost unbroken run from 1274 for six centuries, are a vital source of information about the social and economic life of a considerable, varied and significant area. But the rolls are now very fragile and the only practical way that their contents can be made available to a wide public is for them to be carefully conserved, transcribed and published. The process is demanding and costly, requiring the skills of both conservator and scholar. The Yorkshire Archaeological Society, which now has the care of the rolls, established a section in 1974 to concentrate on their publication.

In 1991, when Wakefield schoolmaster and historian Harold Speak was chairman of the Court Rolls Section, I was invited to join it as publicity officer. In fact I have also organised a series of events to mark the launch of each volume.

Although municipal art galleries were established across England between 1870 and 1914, Wakefield had no public gallery until 1923. But in 1918 the Holmfield estate had been acquired by the Corporation and added to the public park. The park itself had been founded in 1893 when Clarence Park was opened. Thornes Park had been added in 1924. Holmfield itself, the house, was transformed into a museum and art gallery. But it was the museum which flourished rather than the picture collection. There was no money available to buy works of art and the curator had to rely on gifts, on touring exhibitions or on the loan of paintings and drawings from the National Gallery or from long-established collections such as that at the Art Gallery in Leeds.

To address the situation, three local figures set up a permanent art fund. They were led by Alfred Haley, chairman of the worsted-spinning company of Alfred Haley and Sons, who was himself a collector, primarily of Victorian art including works by Ruskin, Burne-Jones, Rossetti and Whistler. A year after Holmfield was opened, Haley suggested forming a society which would acquire art for the new Museum. Although nothing came of this, Haley was shortly afterwards co-opted onto the local authority's Museum sub-committee. There was already another co-opted figure, John Swire, who had come to Wakefield in 1878 as head of the Art School. He had retired in 1920 but remained in Wakefield living at Flower Terrace in Pinderfields Road. He had taken considerable interest in the setting up of art rooms at Holmfield. The third figure behind the permanent art fund was Francis Bush, Inspector of Art for the West Riding Education Authority.

In 1926 Swire bought an Atkinson Grimshaw picture, *Baiting the Lines, Whitby*, for £2 on behalf of the council, seeking retrospective approval from the Museum Sub-Committee. It was a far-sighted start but it was probably the sale of the private collection of art from Lupset Hall in January 1927 that finally prompted the setting up of the Wakefield Permanent Art Fund which led, in turn, to the emergence of the Friends of Wakefield Art Gallery. To mark its seventieth anniversary, I was invited to research and write its history. Among its most significant achievements was the response of artist Henry Moore when, in 1979, the Friends bought *The Fallen Giant*,

Wakefield Art Gallery, Wentworth Terrace. *The author's collection*

one of fifteen lithographs inspired by Stonehenge – Moore donated the whole series to the Art Gallery.

As a trustee of Westgate Chapel, I became a trustee of the Daniel Gaskell foundation in the 1990s. This trust which today makes small grants to Horbury students has its origins in the philanthropy of Daniel Gaskell (1782–1875), the owner of Lupset Hall and, in 1832, when it became a Parliamentary borough, Wakefield's first member of Parliament.

Gaskell's intention was to ensure that the children of Horbury's poor were provided with elementary education free of charge. In 1842 he built a school which children could attend without payment. In those days there was no compulsory education. Such schools as there were, were normally denominational ones, provided by the local Anglican church or by such other bodies as the Methodists or Roman Catholics. Children normally paid a penny or twopence a week to attend. Gaskell's school was different. He was a Unitarian and his school was open to any child whatever the religious beliefs of its family.

When Gaskell died in 1875, the school and the master's house were placed in the hands of the trustees of Westgate Chapel in

Daniel Gaskell, from a portrait at Lupset Hall. *The author*

Wakefield, Gaskell's own spiritual home. Gaskell left an endowment of £1000 in railway stock so that the school could be maintained and the master's salary paid.

The school continued as an elementary school until 1888. But now elementary education had changed radically. By 1880, following the provisions of the 1870 Education Act, school attendance had become compulsory up to at least the age of ten and no child under thirteen could be employed unless they had reached 'standard V'. Children of thirteen who were still below the magical standard had to continue at school as half-timers.

In 1888 the Board of Guardians, taking on the role of a school attendance committee, pointed out that the necessary records were not being kept at Gaskell's school and that its pupils were entering employment illegally. The trustees investigated and realised that the Guardians were right. William Mortimer, the long-standing schoolmaster resigned – but continued to occupy the school-house. For the next six years, the school was run by one of Mortimer's daughters as an infant school. It was then closed. Horbury had four other elementary schools by then, though they were all tied to religious denominations.

For some years the school building deteriorated and the trust funds began to build up. It became clear that the school would never re-open. In 1908 a scheme was agreed with the Government Board of Education for the trust income to be used to give scholarships to secondary-school children going from Horbury to Thornes House in Wakefield or to Ossett School. When these ceased to be fee-paying schools, scholarships were provided for Wakefield Girls' High School and Queen Elizabeth Grammar School. The funds were enhanced in 1957 by a bequest from John Wray. Wray had been a Horbury grocer and in 1892 he was chairman of the Horbury Local Board. It was after his widow died in 1946 that the funds he left for the benefit of Horbury students became available and in due course the Charity Commission suggested that the money might best be handled by the Gaskell trustees. Gaskell's school itself was demolished in 1923.

Today the Gaskell Trust operates under a scheme agreed with the Charity Commission in 1986. Under this, four of the trustees are appointed by the trustees of Westgate Chapel, two are appointed by Wakefield District Council as the education authority, one is appointed by the trustees of the Horbury Educational Foundation, and there is provision for co-optative trustees who have a special knowledge of Horbury. Eddie Walker, for many years the News Editor of the *Wakefield Express*, was one of the first two co-optative trustees. The present chairman, local historian Christine Cudworth, was the other.

Each year the trustees make modest grants to perhaps half-a-dozen or ten students from Horbury who are, normally, in higher education or who, because of a particular talent, are attending a specialist school.

Just occasionally, I have served as press officer for the Gaskell Trust as I have for almost all the other organisations to which I have belonged.

CHAPTER 6

CAMPAIGNS – SUCCESSFUL AND UNSUCCESSFUL

Towns and cities have their individual character, derived from their topography and their buildings. Despite the considerable amount of demolition in the second half of the twentieth century, Wakefield still has some fine historic buildings, among them its remaining churches and chapels, its public buildings in Wood Street, and, in Westgate, its commercial premises and the surviving Georgian town houses.

In the past quarter of a century, I have been involved in a number of campaigns to preserve this local heritage – some quite successful, others entirely fruitless.

My first involvement came in 1975, during European Architectural Heritage Year, when Pemberton House, the Georgian house at the foot of the approach to Westgate Station, was threatened with demolition. The house had been built in 1752–3 for Pemberton Milnes, a Wakefield cloth merchant. Between 1842 and 1864 it had been the home of Henry Clarkson, the author (in his eighties) of *Memories of Merry Wakefield*. Emboldened by the success of the series of articles I had edited and which were then appearing in local papers, I wrote to the *Wakefield Express* voicing concern about the proposal by British Rail. A second letter came from Eric Raper, President of Wakefield Historical Society. The local authority rejected the application but British Rail appealed against the decision and in January 1976 there was a public inquiry. Both Eric Raper and I appeared, arguing for the historic significance of the building itself and for its value as a visual element in the Georgian streetscape. Other conservationists queued up to speak. In April we learned that the appeal had been rejected. Pemberton House had been saved. In the early years of the twenty-first century it has been recognised as a prestige element in proposals for the redevelopment of the Westgate-Balne Lane area.

Situated in the market area, Wakefield's Elizabethan Grammar School is in a vulnerable position and, even though the building itself may be undamaged, its environment at the end of market days is a

Pemberton House, Westgate, in 2005. *The author*

miserable sight, strewn with litter. In the 1960s and 1970s the building itself was seriously at risk. Pressure from the Civic and Historical Societies led to the local authority buying it for use as an exhibition centre. The Grammar School originated in the 1590s in what was then known as the Goodybower. An antiquary, Roger Dodsworth, described it in 1640 as 'a very beautiful house and pleasantly seated on a piece of ground distant a bow shoot of the north from the Church'. By the 1840s its location was far from pleasant. It was 'surrounded by slaughter-houses, dung heaps and the most disreputable and offensive lanes and alleys of the town'.

The Elizabethan Grammar School in Brook Street, 2005. *The author*

In 1855 the school itself moved to its present home in Northgate to the premises opened in 1834 for the West Riding Proprietary School. The Governors of the Wakefield Charities retained the Elizabethan building and transferred its Greencoat School there from its former home in Westgate. But the Greencoat School closed in 1875 and its trust funds were transferred to provide scholarships to the Grammar School. For a time the old building became a furniture store. Then in 1895 its life as a school was renewed when the Cathedral Boys' Elementary School moved there. But it was vacated yet again in 1960 when the school moved to purpose-built premises opposite the park in Thornes Road.

As a 'sweetener' in the campaign to persuade Wakefield District Council to acquire the still-handsome building, the Civic and Historical Societies promised a donation of £1,000 for the landscaping of its surroundings. By then I was the president of the Civic Society and, with the Historical Society's president, Eric Raper, I stood outside the building for the day on Saturday 14

October 1978 to receive donations. The building was formally opened as the Elizabethan Gallery in 1980. In 1994 an exhibition I had devised on the history of theatre in Wakefield was put on there. But on the whole the gallery was not a success and later in the 1990s it was taken over by the Social Services department as a welfare centre.

Wakefield's inner relief road, a dual carriageway running northwards from Kirkgate and bisecting Vicarage Street, was completed as far as Northgate, just south of Howard Street, in 1972. The new local government structure which had come into being in 1974 made the West Yorkshire County Council the highways authority. Wakefield District Council was anxious that the relief road should continue from the Jacob's Well Lane roundabout to Newton Bar although this meant its passing residential areas and across the Grammar School and High School playing fields. But any decision lay in the powers of the county authority. A residents' action group was formed by people living in the College Grove Road area, to oppose the extension, with Ray Perraudin, whose home was in Westfield Park, playing a leading role.

The Civic Society took up the cause. In what the *Wakefield Express* described as 'a new dimension to the relationship between the

Wakefield from the outer side of Marsh Way in 2005. *The author*

governors and the governed', the objectors were invited to 'say their piece' directly to the county councillors. As the Civic Society's president, I spoke at the critical meeting of the Council's Highways and Transportation sub-committee on 24 January 1978. The Action group was represented by Jack Wright. Wakefield District Council, in the persons of Councillor Tom Dando and the Chief Planning Officer, Peter Spawforth, insisted that the road extension was necessary for Wakefield's economic future. Easy movement of traffic was essential if investors were to be attracted to the city. I pointed out that the only times of day when Northgate and Leeds Road were at all busy were at the beginning and end of the Grammar School day. Otherwise it was comparatively quiet. No relief was needed. The M1 and M62, both running very close to Wakefield, kept the bulk of heavy traffic out of Wakefield anyway. The sub-committee promptly decided to reject the road scheme. The Action Group became a

The Theatre Royal and Opera House in 2005. *The author*

longer-term Residents' Association and the area where the relief road would have run was gradually redeveloped for much-needed comparatively low-cost housing close to the city centre.

Wakefield's present theatre, designed by leading architect Frank Matcham, was opened in 1894 on the site of an earlier theatre built in 1776. It was owned by a local man, Benjamin Sherwood, and then by his wife and family. The Sherwoods built a second theatre, the Empire, in Kirkgate. The theatre presented live productions until 1954, relying in its last years on a mixture of touring revues and resident repertory companies. It was acquired in 1947 by Essoldo, a company formed by Solomon Sheckman and based in Tynmouth. For a time it continued to house live shows but in January 1955 it was re-opened as an Essoldo cinema. Shortly afterwards, Sheckman acquired both the nearby Playhouse and the Corn Exchange which housed the Grand Electric.

But the days of cinema-going were, for the time, almost over. The Grand Electric closed after a fire in 1957 and the whole Corn Exchange building was sold to developers in 1962. The Essoldo closed in 1966 and became a bingo hall. It was acquired by the Ladbroke Group in 1973. In 1979 it was listed by the Department of the Environment as Grade II* which meant that no alterations could be made to either its exterior or interior without the consent of the Department. Statutory listing has saved many a building nationally.

The revival of the theatre began in 1981 and owes much to local businessman Sir Rodney Walker, a man with considerable leadership skills and a talent for turning round failing enterprises. Rodney called a public meeting. It brought massive support, especially from amateur groups involved in opera and drama. The local authority and the Yorkshire Weekly Newspaper group also gave their support. I was there as a representative of Wakefield Civic Society and joined the steering committee to assist with press coverage. With Rodney Walker at the helm, events moved quickly. Wakefield Theatre Trust was formed as a subsidiary of the Wakefield Festival Company Ltd, a registered charity and company limited by guarantee. Negotiations with Ladbroke's led to an agreement to buy the theatre for £55,000. An initial payment of £15,000 in May 1982 gave the Trust unfettered access to the theatre and the trustees launched an appeal for £400,000 to complete the purchase and to finance restoration. In July 1982, Featherstone-born Joe Parker, an architect with the

Liverpool-based practice TACP, was chosen to oversee the work. Two months later, Reg Kirk, a native of Batley but then living in Hull, took on the rôle of administrator with the task of raising £100,000. In November 1982 a body of Friends was formed with dual aims of helping with fund-raising and with the practical operation of the theatre.

The rescue of the theatre was an outstanding, and very unusual example of community involvement, certainly one of the most ambitious community projects Wakefield has ever seen. Numbers of Wakefield people played a significant part in raising money and in putting on performances in the still unrestored building or in helping with all manner of practical and administrative tasks. George Littlewood, chairman of the Friends and formerly a road-transport manager with the National Coal Board, who was a member of Wakefield Little Theatre, worked almost full time albeit in a purely voluntary capacity. Serious money came from Wakefield District Council and from the short-lived West Yorkshire County Council which made grants totalling £347,000.

The first performance came in March 1983, appropriately titled *Curtain Up* and staged by the Wakefield West Riding Operatic Society. Wakefield Little Theatre followed with a production of *Hay Fever* in September. Prunella Scales gave an *Evening with Queen Victoria*.

In May 1984 the theatre was closed for refurbishment. In May 1985 the District Council agreed an annual grant for four years, thus allowing the Theatre Trust to appoint a director. Graham d'Albert, who had been the Arts Officer for the West Yorkshire County Council, took up the post on 1 April, 1986. Meanwhile the theatre re-opened on 16 March, 1986 with a variety show designed as a tribute to the County Council which ceased to exist at the end of that month.

Apart from writing many press releases and contributing text to a souvenir brochure, my own contribution was to research and write a history of theatre on the Westgate site. It took ten years of pretty solid work before *Right Royal: Wakefield Theatre 1776–1994* was published in 1995 by Wakefield Historical Publications. It is encouraging to know that plans are in place, in 2005, for an extension to the theatre on the adjacent site which had once been intended, by the Sherwood family, for a music hall.

Wakefield's sole remaining chantry chapel – it was one of four free-standing chantries each lying on a main route into the town – was built in the 1350s at the same time as the stone bridge of which it forms a part. The bridge, still today essentially the same medieval structure, replaced a wooden bridge which had been prone to damage whenever the River Calder was in spate. As well as being a house of prayer, the chantry serves as a buttress to the bridge itself. Although many chantries were endowed by the well-to-do, the chantry on the bridge was financed by the ordinary people of the town. So generous was their provision that it was served by two priests for whom a small dwelling was provided at the northern end of the bridge. For almost two hundred years, it was a place where masses were said for the dead and where, possibly, there were prayers for travellers. The only excitement to be chronicled was the death of the seventeen-year-old Earl of Rutland, Edmund, the son of Richard, Duke of York, who was killed near the chapel by Lord Clifford in 1460 during the Battle of Wakefield.

At the Reformation the chapel was closed under the Act for the Dissolution of Chantries of 1547 and was sold, with its endowments. It passed rapidly through several hands before being acquired by Henry Savile of Lupset. Savile died in 1569 leaving provision in his will for the bridge chapel to become a hospital, or almshouse, for six poor people. Savile's wishes were never carried out but his charitable intent was to some extent fulfilled when the chantry was conveyed in the mid-seventeenth century to the Trustees of the Wakefield Poor. In the next three centuries it was used for many and varied secular purposes for example as a warehouse, a cheesecake shop and a shop for an old-clothes dealer who displayed his garments on the chapel's pinnacles.

The West Riding magistrates – the forerunners of the County Council – were responsible under an act of Parliament of Henry VIII's time for the maintenance of bridges. It seems that the deteriorating state of the chapel was of some real concern to them and in 1797 they leased the building from the Trustees of the Poor. They put repairs in hand which included the insertion of four columns in the front of the chapel. Just as the Trustees had done, the magistrates continued to let the chantry to a variety of tenants.

Then, in the 1830s came the Oxford Movement (sometimes called the Tractarian or Anglo-Catholic Movement) and a whole new existence for the chantry. The Movement was all about reviving practices associated with the medieval Roman Catholic church within the Church of England. It prompted immense interest in medieval church buildings as well as pressure for all new churches to be built in the, supposedly more spiritual, Gothic, rather than Classical style. The Yorkshire Architectural Society, founded in Leeds in 1842, was an off-shoot of the Movement. Amongst its goals was the restoration of 'mutilated medieval remains'. The vicar of Wakefield, Samuel Sharp, joined the Society and proposed at a meeting in the autumn of 1842 that it should undertake the restoration of the chapel on Wakefield Bridge. Members responded with enthusiasm, though not, perhaps with much wisdom. Sharp, who was himself one of the Governors of the Wakefield Charities, was able to persuade the Trustees to give (not sell!) the bridge chapel to the church authorities. Speaking at Quarter Sessions, he persuaded the magistrates to give up their lease. In a letter to the Ecclesiastical Commissioners, he asked them to accept the chapel and offered to pay for the conveyancing himself.

In early 1843 the Yorkshire Architectural Society announced a competition for architects to submit a scheme for the restoration of the chantry. Designs were submitted anonymously. The winning one proved to be by George Gilbert Scott. Lamentably, Scott proposed to dismantle the medieval building to pavement level and to build a new Gothic chapel in its place. The beautifully sculpted front was sold to George Chapple Norton of Kettlethorpe Hall and became an attraction at the side of the lake in his grounds. Scott's new chantry was opened at Easter 1848. In 1844, two areas of the parish of Wakefield were separated off to become the new ecclesiastical districts of St Andrew's and St Mary's. The chantry lay within the boundaries of St Mary's. When it was re-opened, it served as the parish church until the new church, at Primrose Hill, was opened in 1854. It was then – after all the effort on the part of Samuel Sharp – effectively redundant, and, worse than that, it rapidly became a serious burden to the impoverished parish. The stone Scott imported for his chapel eroded rapidly in the acid air of industrial Wakefield. The first major repairs became necessary in the early 1880s. Further costly repairs in the late 1930s included the complete replacement of Scott's front by one designed by Sir Charles Nicholson.

Slum clearance in the years after the Second World War took away much of the population of St Mary's parish and it was merged with the neighbouring St Andrew's in 1966. St Mary's Church was

The medieval chantry front in the grounds of Kettlethorpe Hall in 1949. *Ron Head*

demolished. But St Andrew's Parochial Church Council became responsible for the chantry which was again deteriorating badly and which was closed between 1969 and 1971 for major repairs. In the 1980s, led by the new vicar, Reverend Bryan Ellis, St Andrew's tried to rid itself of its burdensome chapel. It tried to interest the National Trust, the Redundant Churches Fund, English Heritage and Wakefield District Council to take over responsibility for it. None would do so and, indeed, Wakefield Historical Society opposed any take-over by the Council on the grounds of its poor record in regard to other old buildings.

The Civic Society convened a meeting in November 1990 to try to resolve St Andrew's problem. It was attended by representatives of

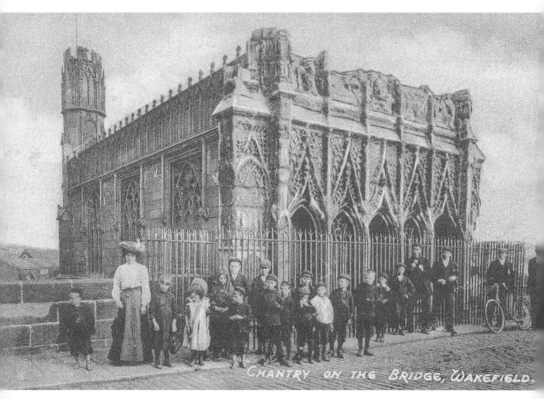

The chantry in the early years of the twentieth century showing the erosion of George Gilbert Scott's front. *The Friends of Wakefield Chantry Chapel*

the local authority, the Wakefield diocese, the Historical Society, Churches Together in Wakefield, the Chantry Lodge of Freemasons, and St Andrew's PCC. Capably steered by John Gilbey, an agreement was reached to establish a body of Friends which would raise funds for the care and maintenance of the chapel and would also make it known to a wider public. I joined the management committee as, unsurprisingly, the press officer. The Lady St Oswald, the Bishop of Wakefield, and the Right Honourable Walter Harrison agreed to become patrons. We set out to raise £100,000. We held – and still hold – open days at public-holiday weekends but we also wanted to see the chantry used for talks, music and drama. In 1993, Wakefield Flower Club staged a festival there with arrangements symbolising local industries. A few weeks later Audrey Cauldron,

The chantry in 1939 with the newly erected third front. *The author's collection*

who had been head of drama at Bretton Hall College, appeared in the chantry as the first Queen Elizabeth in her own play, *King Harry's Daughter.*

John Gilbey was determined that restoration work should begin as quickly as possible. By 1994 the roof had been repaired and in 1995 the building was fully re-wired with new lighting and heating systems installed. In 1996 scaffolding was erected and extensive repairs were made to the stonework. Six new label stops, the external stone heads at the sides of each window, were sculpted on the south side. They portrayed the then Bishop of Wakefield, Nigel McCullough, the vicar of St Andrew's, Bryan Ellis, Lady St Oswald, Ray Perraudin who was the first secretary of the Friends, Walter Harrison, and an anonymous stonemason.

On two occasions Arthur Starkie gave his own one-man dramas, *Uneasy Lies the Head,* based on the life of Charles I, and *This Son of*

Arthur Starkie as Charles I. *The author's collection*

York, portraying Richard III in the chapel. Arthur was an amazing man. He spent twenty-four years as a drama teacher at Thornes House before becoming Head of Drama at the Cathedral School. After his retirement he devised the two plays and performed them at heritage sites across the country. He also built detailed models of theatres; his model of Shakespeare's Globe was exhibited at the Shakespeare Centre in Stratford-upon-Avon. In May 1998 he was diagnosed with motor neurone disease and he died in 1999.

Although the Friends attended to the physical state of the chantry, the provision of services remained the responsibility of St Andrew's. It was often urged that it should be in the care of the Cathedral Chapter rather than the parish which had acquired it by an accident of history. The appointment of George Nairn-Briggs as Provost of Wakefield in 1997 brought a sympathetic figure to the cause. At the beginning of 2000 an Order in Council changed the boundaries of

The Archbishop of York, the Most Reverend Dr David Hope, at the chantry in September 2003. *The author*

the parishes of St Andrew's, Thornes, and Wakefield itself, and the Chantry was taken into the care of the Dean and Chapter of Wakefield at much the same time as changes at the Cathedral made George Nairn-Briggs its Dean.

John Gilbey died in 2001 and I became the chair of the Friends. We reached the £100,000 target early in 2003. The achievement was marked by a service in the Chantry on 4 September, 2003 when the then Archbishop of York gave the address. The Most Reverend Dr David Hope is a Wakefield lad. He lived in Thornes Lane and went to Queen Elizabeth Grammar School. He returned to Wakefield as its Bishop in November 1985 before going on to the Diocese of London and then to York. We had a dinner at the *Cedar Court Hotel* after the service and, seated between Dr Hope and the Mayor of Wakefield, David Atkinson, I had the fun of listening to them sharing their memories of Wakefield in the war.

After his father's death and the dowager Lady St Oswald's leaving the district, the present Lord St Oswald (Charles) accepted our invitation to become a patron. He proposed our raising funds by holding a bridge tournament in 2003 at Nostell Priory. It was a delightful, as well as financially modestly successful event. Although no bridge player, I had a highly enjoyable evening in a small sitting room on the same floor as the tournament, chatting with the Dean of Wakefield, George Nairn-Briggs, and Charles St Oswald.

Among our fund-raising efforts was the creation and sale of picture-postcards. This began when an avid postcard collector, Alan Bower, who occasionally published postcards himself, gave us a set of cards picturing the chantry. We then obtained some sponsorship from Pearl Assurance plc and created our own cards from photographs taken by Barry Jackson of the Wakefield Camera Club, A P Oldroyd, and John Newton. We wanted further views of the Chantry and my own first venture was a shot of the south side of the Chantry from the bank of the Calder. No other body seemed to be producing new Wakefield postcards and the Tourist Information Centre was willing to take a wider range from the Friends. My most hair-raising experience was to photograph the Cathedral and the pedestrian precinct from the flat roof of Boots in Upper Kirkgate. This involved climbing a vertical metal ladder on the outside of the topmost part of the building and leaning out over the parapet. But the resulting shot was well worth it.

Wakefield Cathedral taken from the roof of Boots. *The author*

Not So Merry Wakefield

Once the excavations of 1964–73 were complete, the Sandal Castle site was left unattended, its stonework now exposed. It was to remain a place for much dog-walking and for children to play. Children – and young adults too – used the grassed slopes of the motte for slides or as mountain-bike tracks. Wakefield Historical Society began to call for conservation and supervision almost immediately and year after year its annual meeting heard its officers condemn the local authority for their neglect.

After years of pressure from the Society, the then Leisure Services department of Wakefield Council set up a working group in the early 1990s to explore the way forward for the Castle. It included representatives of English Heritage and the West Yorkshire Archaeological Service as well as council officers. I joined it as the representative of the Historical Society. Its report was completed in 1993. At last, in 2002, access was provided to the courtyard and the top of the motte by a new wooden footbridge and steps. A modest visitor centre was opened at the same time. The problem of vandalism, with stones regularly pushed from the castle walls into the moat, has never been solved.

Sandal Castle in 2005 showing the new bridge and access steps to the top of the motte. *The author*

For almost 150 years, the medieval front of Wakefield's bridge chantry stood beside the lake at Kettlethorpe Hall. But during that period Kettlethorpe itself changed. The Hall was acquired by Wakefield Council in 1950. It became a residential home for the elderly. The lake became a venue for anglers. The local authority's housing estate was built to the west of the Hall in the 1950s and Kettlethorpe School was opened close to the grounds of the Hall in 1965. There was concern from then on for the preservation of the

The vandalised front of the medieval chantry in 1993. *The author*

front. In 1977 the short-lived Conservation Executive Group asked that the Chief Architect suggest an appropriate treatment to preserve the stones.

The residential home closed in 1983 and Kettlethorpe Hall itself was bought by the Yorkshire Preservation Trust in 1988 and was reinstated and converted into two houses. The lake and grounds, however, remained in local authority control. From 1991, the beautiful medieval stonework of the chantry, which was listed as an ancient monument, became a target for vandals. In 1993 the damage was becoming marked. Wakefield Historical Society alerted the local authority and urged it to give the building some protection. In July the Society passed a resolution condemning the council for its neglect. Councillors, seemingly more concerned about the dangers to children of falling masonry than about a precious relic, supported either the removal of the structure and its rebuilding in a safer place or conservation on its present site. In the event, the stones were removed and put into storage, and there in 2005 they remain.

Vandalism and a lack of care, will, or money on the part of the local authority meant that Wakefield lost a remarkable medieval relic.

CHAPTER 7

SEVENTY YEARS OF CHANGE

The Wakefield I knew as a child has gone. It has lost something of its physical character and much of its status. Wakefield became a municipal borough in 1848 with a mayor and elected councillors. The corporation was, perhaps, always short sighted, almost always afraid to spend ratepayers' money, and hence it did nothing to stop the increasing regional domination of Leeds. Cheese-paring in the 1850s and 1860s, when councillors drew the line at building a town hall, meant that when the West Riding got its own Assizes, separately from the County Assizes hitherto held in York, it was Leeds – largely because of its splendid town hall – that gained the new courts and all the economic advantage they brought. As just another example, long after other authorities had provided an alternative to burial – and Wakefield funerals were going to Leeds – Wakefield opened its crematorium, at Kettlethorpe, in October 1961.

Wakefield became a County Borough in 1915. This gave it powers, inter alia, over secondary education in addition to those it had had since 1902 for elementary education.

Wakefield crematorium in 2005. *The author*

But from 1889 Wakefield was the home of the newly-created West Riding County Council. This was part of a further step nationally on the road to democracy as elected bodies took on many of the responsibilities held for centuries by the justices of the peace. The splendid County Hall was built in Wood Street in the 1890s, opening on 22 February 1898. And the West Riding brought men (usually men!) of high calibre into its administration, figures like the great education officer, Sir Alec Clegg, who were of national significance. Many such people made their homes in Wakefield. They brought something of a cultural leaven to Wakefield society.

Local government reorganisation arrived in 1974. Wakefield lost its administrative independence and became part of a metropolitan district covering an area that included Castleford, Hemsworth, Horbury, Normanton and Ossett and all places between. This resulted in a council made up of elected representatives of places other than Wakefield itself which had their own distinctive culture and needs, councillors who might well lack the commitment to Wakefield itself which – whatever their failings – the earlier Wakefield members had. The great West Riding County Council was abolished and with it the administrative area that had stretched from Skipton to Sheffield, from Goole to Todmorden. Yorkshire was re-divided into South, West and North (with the East Riding largely subsumed in the new area of Humberside) and a new West Yorkshire County Council was formed covering the metropolitan districts of Bradford, Calderdale (centred on Halifax), Kirklees (centred on Huddersfield), Leeds and Wakefield.

The new West Yorkshire County Council continued to meet at the County Hall in Wood Street but the Conservative government of 1983–87 decided that it was an unnecessary luxury and it was disbanded in 1986 after a mere twelve years. The West Yorkshire joint services were born, with responsibility for analytical services, archaeology, archives, calibration, grants, materials testing and trading standards in all five authorities still being held by a single over-arching body.

In the first part of the twentieth century the major changes in Wakefield lay in slum clearance and the development of local authority housing estates. Wakefield's first council houses were built in 1920 at Rufford Street, Alverthorpe, and Elm Tree Street, Belle Vue. Then came the great Lupset estate of the 1920s and 1930s, and the Eastmoor and Darnley estates of the 1930s. The Second World

War put a stop to development of any sort but the expansion of council housing, on virgin sites at the perimeter of the city, continued from 1946 with new estates at Flanshaw and Kettlethorpe and an extension of the Eastmoor estate. Wakefield had come late into the field of council house provision (as it came late into so much else) but the houses that the corporation eventually built were something they could take a pride in. Most were semi-detached with gardens to the front and rear. The estates were laid out in an informal manner with crescents and intimate cul-de-sacs and with plenty of open spaces in front of or behind the houses.

The city centre began to change radically in the 1950s. Its core, the Bull Ring, was redeveloped with the widening of the bottom of Northgate by some fifteen feet on its eastern side and new ranges of shops on the corner of Union Street. Until the 1950s the principal town-centre bus stops were in the Bull Ring, the Springs and at the top of Westgate. In September 1952, however, Wakefield's first bus station was opened in Union Street. It lasted a mere half century and was always cold and, within a few years of its opening, very dank and dirty. A replacement was built in 2001.

The distinctive Wakefield skyline, formed in the nineteenth century when the tower of the Town Hall and the dome of County

The Bull Ring in 2004. *The author*

147

The Bull Ring in the early 1950s. *The John Goodchild Collection*

Hall complemented the parish church spire, began to change in the 1950s too. Following the nationalisation of the electricity industry in 1948, the old Wakefield power station was replaced by a much larger one on the opposite side of the river, at Heath. Work began on this in July 1952 and it was formally opened in October 1957. For many years its twin cooling towers formed a part of the Wakefield skyscape. But the station was decommissioned in 1991 and in December of that year the cooling towers were demolished. The power station itself was blown up in June 1994.

One landmark feature was lost when Westgate Station, first opened a hundred years earlier, was rebuilt in 1967 but without its clock tower.

Arguably the first major visual despoliation of the city came with the culture that built upwards. By the 1960s Wakefield Corporation had abandoned its policy of semi-detached and semi-rural council houses and bungalows and had begun to build high-rise council flats close to the centre of town, in George Street and Kirkgate, radically

The entrance to Wakefield's first bus station. *The John Goodchild Collection*

altering the skyline. Carr House was the first block to be opened, in January 1961. Further blocks were built in the suburbs just off Horbury Road.

But councils have long abandoned the policy of building either houses or flats to let. From the late 1970s onwards some houses were

Westgate, showing the railway station clock in the distance. *Wakefield Historical Publications*

sold to individual tenants under the Conservative 'right-to-buy' policy; then in March 2005 the whole of Wakefield's council-housing stock was transferred to Wakefield and District Housing.

Flats were built for modest rents, under a housing association scheme, in the New Wells development, Thornhill Street, in 1982. Affordable housing in the form of flats and a hostel for single people at the junction of Marsh Way and Northgate was provided by the English Churches Housing Association between Marsh Way, Northgate and Arundel Street in 1994.

Large private housing estates developed in the second half of the twentieth century, first on greenfield sites and then, additionally, where collieries, textile mills or hospitals had once stood. The Broom Hall estate, off Bradford Road, was put up for sale in 1938 but development was delayed until after the second world war. Open space in Horbury Road between the site of the Empire Stores and the M1 motorway was developed from 1965. After a three-day public inquiry in 1968 there were vast developments on the Sandal Grange estate and at Pledwick Lane despite objections that they were on good agricultural land and that they would erode the open space between Sandal and Walton. The Pinder's Heath development came in the 1970s.

The housing at the top of Marsh Way in 2005. *The author*

Snapethorpe was the first local hospital to be closed. This was, of course, a triumph for a health service that had seen almost the last of tuberculosis and, because of modern treatment, the removal of risk from diphtheria and scarlet fever. It closed in 1984 and privately-owned houses and flats have been built there since then as well as a private residential home. In 1987, the County General Hospital, which had originated as the workhouse infirmary and had been used by the local authority since 1972 for the care of the elderly, closed. The site again became a private housing development. Stanley Royd Hospital closed in 1995 and a major development of town houses and flats took its place in the first years of the present century.

Voluntary enterprise in 1982 set in motion the scheme for different, but much-needed, nursing care at Wakefield Hospice. Its first patient was admitted in April 1990. It has proved a community triumph.

The supermarket reached Wakefield in the 1960s. The first was Hillard's in Providence Street. Asda's Queen's discount centre opened in the newly-built Kirkgate Way in 1969. There was parking in the adjoining multi-storey car park. A year later, on 10 November 1970, Jimmy Savile opened what it claimed was the 'largest Tesco store in the North' at what was to develop as the junction of Marsh Way and Kirkgate. Neatly removing at least some of the competition, Tesco took over the Hillard's supermarket in Providence Street in 1988. Meanwhile the Co-operative Retail Services Ltd opened Leo's supermarket on land lying between Dewsbury and Horbury Road on 20 June 1974.

Wakefield Hospice in 2005. *The author*

The Ridings shopping centre. *The author*

The Ridings Shopping Centre opened in October 1983. Here, for the first time Wakefield gained a branch of W H Smith's. And, of course, as a modern shopping mall, it had to have a supermarket. Morrison's opened in there on 15 November 1983, a stone's throw from Tesco. Asda moved to Durkar a week later, providing Wakefield's first out-of-town supermarket. There were plans to extend the Ridings Centre, in particular with the addition of a Debenham's department store, taking in an additional part of Southgate, including the offices of the Wakefield Express and the *Spaniard* public house, but the scheme fell through when it failed to secure an Urban Development grant.

Ings Road was widened and became a dual carriageway in 1976. The southern side began to develop with warehouse-style stores earning the local term 'shed city'. Sainsbury's opened a supermarket at the junction of Ings Road and Denby Dale Road on 1 March 1988. The competition proved too much for Tesco which had only a comparatively modest site and it closed on 12 September 1992.

It took Morrison's fifteen years from an initial planning application in 1978 until 18 May 1993 before it could open its store on the site of Westgate Brickworks in Dewsbury Road. Persistent applications were refused, with refusal being confirmed at the company's appeals. Its proximity to Leo's was one of the arguments against it and soon after it opened, Leo's was closed. A Netto supermarket took its chance with the Leo's site in 2000.

The towncentre's intimate street pattern was quite brutally affected when Marsh Way, designed as an inner relief road and some three-quarters of a mile in length, was opened from Northgate to Lower Kirkgate on 25 January 1972. It was named after Alderman James Marsh, a long-serving member of the Wakefield borough council. Effectively it cut off the north-eastern part of the city, bisecting Warrengate, Vicarage Street and York Street. Monstrous concrete underpasses, hailed at the time as a great boon and reviled ever since, allowed pedestrians to walk into town from Peterson Road, Stanley Road, Pinderfields Road, and Saville Street.

Since the inner relief road took much of the through traffic away from the town centre, pedestrianisation was introduced in May 1975 with Upper Kirkgate, Little Westgate, Cross Square, Bread Street and parts of Southgate and Teall Street closed to vehicles and Westmorland Street reserved for buses and taxis.

The monument on Batley Road to the men who died in the Lofthouse Colliery disaster pictured in 2004. *The author*

Coalmining was always dangerous work and perhaps young men have cause to be grateful that it is, at least in Yorkshire, a thing of the past. In the most recent disaster, on 21 March 1973, seven men were killed at Lofthouse Colliery when water from old and uncharted workings inundated the area where they were.

Old Roundwood Colliery, just west of Broadway and quite close to our Flanshaw Lane home, closed in 1966 as did the West Riding Colliery at Lower Altofts. The last coal at Crigglestone Colliery was brought to the surface on 26 April 1968. East Ardsley and Whitwood Collieries closed at much the same time. Walton Colliery closed in December 1979. Manor Colliery went in January 1982, its site on Cross Lane redeveloped for housing. Parkhill Colliery, no great distance from where I had come to live, closed in December of the same year. I was among many who joined a protest march to save Sharlston Colliery but it, too, closed in 1993.

The protest walk at Sharlston Colliery. *The author*

Then came the industrial and retail estates, no doubt important to the local economy as sources of employment and revenue but far from pretty. The opening of the M1 and M62, the widening of Denby Dale Road, and the dual carriageway by-passing the old Bradford Road, fostered these. The first of them, Junction 41, was begun in 1980. Its Business Park opened in 1989. Yorkshire Water was one of the first major organisations to take premises there in 1992.

The late 1990s saw the redevelopment of land to the south of Ings Road as retail 'parks' complete with a multiplex cinema, built by the Cineworld chain, and the ubiquitous fast-food cabins, MacDonald's and Pizza Hut. They are entirely without character and might be anywhere in Britain!

The riverside site to the south of Denby Dale Road, now named Calder Island, was formerly the premises of Hodgson and Simpson's soap works. Abtech and the Calder Island Development Company submitted plans in 1996 for the development of the thirty-five acres for retail and leisure. A cinema and a marina were envisaged. Neither has materialised and with Cineworld only a mile away on the Westgate Retail Park the cinema would have had uncomfortable competition. In fact motor-car showrooms were the first premises to be built there, in 1998.

The 'Westgate run' developed in the 1980s. It could be argued that the conversion of one building after another into a fun-pub has been

Westgate Retail Park in 2005. *The author*

Cineworld, Westgate Retail Park 2005. *The author*

a means of saving noble buildings that would otherwise have stood empty and deteriorating. But it has also meant that for many, on Friday and Saturday evenings in particular, Westgate is a 'no go' area as herds of inebriated, and scantily-clad youngsters swarm the streets

The *Great Bull Hotel*, which was built in the 1770s and was once Wakefield's foremost inn, as part of the Westgate night-club scene, in 2005. *The author*

The *Chasley Hotel* in 2005. *The author*

roaming from one venue to another. Banners frequently deface the buildings, concealing their architectural detail, advertising cheap drinks. Fast-food outlets result in litter and greasy pavements. Banks and a law firm which gave Westgate some continuing gravitas and daytime activity, moved out or are planning to do so, leaving a main route into the city with little daytime activity.

The first modern hotel in Wakefield was the *Metropolitan* which opened just off Queen Street in 1965 and was renamed subsequently as *Cesar's*, the *Swallow*, and the *Chasley Hotel*. Several of the houses making up Stoneleigh Terrace at Agbrigg were converted into the *Stoneleigh* hotel in 1976. Later hotels were built on the outskirts of Wakefield closer to the M1 motorway. The *Albany* was built at Roundwood in 1972 and become the *Post House* in February 1977 when it was taken into the Trust House Forte chain. Later it became the *Holiday Inn. Cedar Court*, on Denby Dale Road, was financed in

The *Hotel Campanile* at the side of the Aire and Calder Navigation, 2005. *The author*

part by the Wakefield textile concern, Sirdar, and the Sirdar group director, Jean Tyrrel, performed the topping-out ceremony in October 1984. It opened in 1985. Sirdar relinquished its interest in 1997. The *Campanile,* close to the Aire and Calder Navigation at Thornes, opened in 1992. Strand Hotels opened the *St Pierre* at Newmillerdam in the same year. Ten years later the *Express,* another Holiday Inn development, was opened at the Calder Park on Denby Dale Road. *Day's Hotel,* close to the M1 on the unattractive Silkwood Industrial Park, was opened in 2004.

By the end of the twentieth century, Wakefield had lost much of its traditional economic base. Kilner's, the glass manufacturers in Calder Vale Road, closed in October 1954. It had produced goods primarily for the chemical industry including carboys. Its site was taken over by Edward Green's. This, too, closed in 2005.

The strength of sterling in the 1990s made exporting difficult and cheap imports added to the problems of Wakefield's textile industry. M P Stonehouse's Albion Mills, at the junction of Westgate and Ings Road, closed in October 1997. The firm had been founded in 1854 and produced yarns for the worsted industry. In the years prior to closure it had become part of the Readicut International group. Although the Georgian houses in which the firm had originated have been retained, the mill complex was demolished in 1998 and retail premises were built on the site.

Another worsted-spinning firm Alfred Haley's, founded in 1886, closed in April 1999. Its site was taken for another residential development.

Charles Roberts had founded his engineering firm at Horbury Bridge in 1852. It was taken over by Thomas Carmichael of Wolverhampton in 1993 and closed down almost immediately. Bradley and Craven's was established in Dewsbury Road in 1843 by Richard Bradley and William Craven who had been apprentice engineers at Edward Green's in Calder Vale Road. The firm manufactured agricultural implements, steam engines and colliery winding gear. Most importantly, perhaps, it went on to produce brick-making machinery with a design patented in 1853 which revolutionised the brick-making process. In 1972 the company merged with Thomas C Fawcett of Leeds to become Craven Fawcett. It went into liquidation in 2001. Three years later the premises were demolished to be replaced by car showrooms.

British Jeffrey Diamond began in 1897, Queen Victoria's diamond-jubilee year, as the Diamond Coal-cutting Company and was founded by Sir William Garforth. It merged with the American

Heath Old Hall. *The John Goodchild Collection*

Jeffrey Manufacturing Company in 1928, changing its name at the same time. In 1974 it became part of Dresser Industries but by then the decline in the coal industry meant that the writing was on the wall. A management buy-out in 1990 failed to save it and it went into liquidation in 2000.

The twentieth century saw the end of almost all of Wakefield's suburban mansions and country houses as family homes. I hold no particular brief for the aristocracy or the gentry but nonetheless love some of the great houses they built and have been grieved at their neglect, inappropriate uses or demise. Some came into the care of local authorities. Others, like the Elizabethan Heath Old Hall and Newland Hall, were demolished. Newland was the victim of industrialisation; its aristocratic owners moved to another rural estate to escape the railways and sold it in the 1860s to colliery owners; St John's Colliery nearby was opened in 1870 ensuring an end to gracious living. The Hall fell into ruin and was blown up in 1917. Heath Old Hall was demolished in 1961.

Walton Hall is one of the most romantic of country houses, not least because it is surrounded by a lake. The estate had belonged to the Waterton family since the mid fifteenth century and the present hall was built in 1767–8 by Thomas Waterton, father of the traveller and naturalist, Charles. It was Charles Waterton who turned the grounds into the world's first nature reserve and who surrounded

Walton Hall in 2004. *The author*

them with a vast stone wall, a part of which runs beside the Barnsley Canal. Walton Hall became a maternity hospital in 1942. Women in labour had no option but to walk across the iron footbridge to its island site. Extensions at Manygates Maternity Hospital in 1966 led to its closure and the Hall then became a residential home for the elderly. That too closed. In 1970 the Hall was bought for £12,000 from Earnshaw's, the timber merchants, by local businessmen David Hulme and Peter Carney. Later Hulme bought Carney out for a further £10,000. That Walton Hall still stands, handsomely, today is due to Hulme's investment there. His main interest, however, lay in the forty-acre lake as a facility for water-skiing. The lake was badly silted from nearby open-cast mining but was dredged. Both Hulme's children, Kathryn and Robert, practised there and became sufficiently expert to join British national teams. In 1982 Kathryn set a world record in water-ski jumping which remained unbeaten for twenty years.

At first under Hulme's ownership the Hall itself was left largely untouched except for the provision of hot water, a bath and a lavatory for the skiers. Initially in 1973, he proposed to demolish the house and replace it with a sports centre. But interest in the architectural qualities of country houses was quickening and opposition proved too great. Instead the Hall itself became a country club with a membership peaking at 4,000. Hulme spent £1 million on its renovation. He built the swimming pool and café-bar at the rear of the Hall and built squash courts on the 'mainland'. There were happy days with a family-orientated atmosphere and occasional barbecues and even raft races. But Hulme's company, Milthorpe International, and the club, went into receivership in 1983. For a time the club remained open but, with no buyer in prospect, it closed in January 1984. The extensive contents of the wine cellar, including spirits and champagne, were auctioned the same month. Three months later the Hall and its estate were bought by Keith Manners, a Batley man whose father had been chairman of the Ralph Cuthbert chain of chemists and who owned hotels in Jersey. It was reopened as *Walton Hall Hotel*. Then in October 1988 David and Deidre Kaye from Beverley called in for coffee. They liked what they saw and made an offer for it. They acquired the Hall in April 1989 and rebranded it as *Waterton Park Hotel*. It remains a prestigious venue for conferences and weddings.

Hatfeild Hall, dating from the beginning of the seventeenth century and home from 1898 to 1917 to solicitor Herbert Beaumont, was sold by his heirs to the West Riding Asylums Board and became a home to women with mental disabilities. When Fieldhead Hospital was opened in 1972, it was no longer required for that purpose and became the administrative headquarters of the Wakefield district of the Area Health Authority. It came on the market in 1982 and was eventually bought by Jayme Fernandes and Sean McMaster. In 1985 they opened it as a leisure centre. There was a disastrous fire, attributed to arson, on 1 January 1987, which was followed by thieving and vandalism. The Hall was boarded up and became increasingly derelict. However in the early 1990s it was bought by Normanton Golf Club. The house was restored, albeit without the fine panelling and decorated plaster ceiling in the principal rooms, and is run by the club as a restaurant and conference centre whilst the grounds have been laid out as a golf course. The coach-house remains a ruin.

Holmfield was inhabited by a series of Wakefield 'worthies': it was built in 1833 for a solicitor, Thomas Foljambe; between 1863 and 1892, Major Joseph Barker, a worsted spinner, lived there; finally it was the home of a draper, Alderman W H Kingswell. After Kingswell's death, Wakefield Corporation bought Holmfield and its grounds in 1918 and added it to the public park. The house was used

Hatfeild Hall in 2005. *The author*

The coach house, Hatfeild Hall in 2005. *The author*

from 1923 as a municipal art gallery and museum. After the opening of the Art Gallery in Wentworth Terrace in 1934 and the City Museum in Wood Street in the 1940s it became a favourite venue for wedding receptions, its magnificent rockery providing a backdrop for the photographs. After local government re-organisation it was managed by the local authority's Recreation and Amenities Department and was modernised, with a new lounge bar, in 1976, in the hope that it would be used for conferences and exhibitions as well as wedding receptions and other private parties. It was refitted and relaunched in December 1982 with rooms now named after Thomas Foljambe and the Castleford-born sculptor, Henry Moore. It was not a financial success and ten years later it was closed to be leased to Whitbread's. Despite local opposition – including that of the Civic Society – a massive extension was built to provide a forty-two bedroom hotel. The rockery, which had by then been much vandalised, was bulldozed in December 1994. Two Wakefield relics were rescued from the rockery: a column from the Market Cross which was demolished in 1866 and an eleven-foot high pinnacle which was removed from the parish church (now the cathedral) during repairs in the 1860s. They were no doubt added to the rockery by Major Barker. They were taken to the garden of the Art Gallery in Wentworth Terrace.

The adjoining Thornes House estate had been inherited in 1873 by Charles George Milnes Gaskell, first chairman of the West Riding County Council. He died in 1919 and the property was put on the market. Again the buyer was Wakefield Corporation but this time the Council wanted it for a secondary school and municipal housing. Thornes House did, in fact, become a secondary grammar school but its lake, formal gardens and parkland made a final addition to the public park. The house, which dated from the 1780s and had been designed by John Carr, was destroyed by fire in 1951.

Seeking open land for development as housing estates, Wakefield Corporation bought the Snapethorpe Hall estate in 1926. The house was used for some years as a community centre and children's welfare clinic and part of its gardens was let as a horticultural nursery. It was later demolished.

Lupset Hall, home in the nineteenth century of Wakefield's first member of Parliament, Daniel Gaskell, ceased to be in private ownership in 1927 when it too was bought by Wakefield Corporation. It became the club house for the municipal golf club. Some of the land was acquired by Empire Stores.

Alverthorpe Hall was demolished in 1946. Flanshaw First School was opened on its site in 1949. That same year Flanshaw Hall, which had been bought by the Corporation from Marjorie Wolstenholme, was demolished to make way for Flanshaw St Michael's Junior School.

Woolley Hall, dating from the first half of the seventeenth century and owned by members of the Wentworth family, was bought by the West Riding County Council in 1947 and converted to provide residential courses, primarily for the in-service training of teachers.

Wakefield Corporation bought Chevet Hall from the Pilkington family in 1949. Initially, Wakefield had planned to use it – most unsuitably – as a home for boys with handicaps. However the cost of conversion was prohibitive. In 1955 the Hall was sold to Job Earnshaw and Sons, the timber merchants, of Midgley. Finally, it was sold to S H Demolition of Bradford. A two-day sale of its fixtures and fittings was held in July 1955. Whatever could be taken away was offered among the 600 or so lots – doors, windows, a staircase, stone flags, oak flooring, and much more. A cheese press was bought for

Wakefield Museum. Among the treasures was a Portland stone fireplace bearing the date 1761 which had been retrieved from the grounds having been taken out of the Hall during renovations fifty years earlier.

Heath Hall had been used as a military hospital during the First World War. After standing empty for many years, it was used by the army in the Second World War. It then became a hostel for refugees and was subsequently leased by the West Riding County Council for use for its County Supplies Department. In 1959 Mary and Muir Oddie, who primarily wanted the farm land for their horses, bought the Hall as well as its estate. Years of careful restoration followed for which Mary was awarded an OBE. But Muir died in 1978 and Mary put the house on the market. It was bought by John Cook, a dealer in Italian furniture, who used it for some time as showrooms. However in 1985 it was up for sale again. The Purbic Group of Sunningdale, Berkshire, was interested, proposing to use it for management training courses. It seemed that the Hall would never be used as a family home again. However, when Purbic Northern went into liquidation, the Hall was bought from the receivers by Terry Hodgkinson and he and his wife Ann and their daughters

Mary and Muir Oddie. *The John Goodchild Collection*

Clarke Hall in the 1970s. *The author's collection*

went to live there. They sold it in 2003 to Anthony and Vivienne Hodges.

In 1954 Crofton Old Hall became a secondary modern school.

Clarke Hall was last inhabited by Henry Charlesworth Haldane but after his death in 1967 it was acquired by the West Riding County Council, prompted primarily by Ray Perraudin, and was opened in 1971 as an educational museum.

Bretton Hall was acquired by the West Riding County Council and opened as a teacher-training college in 1949. In 1993, under the principalship of Dr Gordon Bell, the college 'invaded' Wakefield. In 1993 its Powerhouse Theatre and studio were opened in Smyth Street. A year later it took over Colonial Buildings, built for the provision merchants, Dysons, in Peterson Road in 1907, and renamed it Powerhouse 2. Studio 23 was a conversion of premises in Smyth Street for art work. Then in 1995 the college bought the disused Manygates Maternity Hospital and, erecting many new buildings, turned it into a student village. Financially the college was badly overstretched. Colonial Buildings was sold to Magna Holdings to be refurbished as studios and offices. The future of both Bretton Hall and the college's other Wakefield sites is, in 2005, in serious doubt.

The visitor centre, Yorkshire Sculpture Park, in 2004. *The author*

In a separate development the Yorkshire Sculpture Park was founded in the grounds of Bretton Hall, opening in September 1977. In 2002 a new access road was provided and the Visitor Centre opened in June 2002. The centre was designed by Fielden Clegg, an architectural practice in which Clegg, the son of the West Riding Education Officer, Sir Alec Clegg, was a partner. My younger sister generously paid for my name to be included in the 'Walk of Art' pathway to the Visitor Centre entrance. An ambitious underground gallery was opened in May 2005.

The demise of country houses and the death of coal mining have brought considerable benefits to

The author finding her name in the Walk of Art, Yorkshire Sculpture Park 2004. *The author's collection*

The boathouse and lake, Newmillerdam, 2004. *The author*

Wakefield at least in the way of places to walk. Newmillerdam lake
and woods had been a part of the Pilkington family's Chevet Hall
estate. Wakefield Corporation bought 178 acres, including the lake,
in 1954 for public recreational use. Its boathouse, dating probably

Geese enjoying one of the lakes at Walton Country Park in 2005. *The author*

from the 1820s was listed in 1967 but stood almost derelict until the 1990s when grants from, among others, the Heritage Lottery Fund, saw it fully restored and made available for meetings, exhibitions and other events.

Shortly after its creation in 1974, the West Yorkshire County Council bought ten hectares of despoiled land on Lime Pit Lane at Stanley. Here the work to create Stanley Marsh Nature Reserve from the swamp, scrub and woodland, was undertaken primarily by the British Trust for Conservation volunteers. Disused mine shafts were capped and a raised wooden walkway was created. The area was formally opened on 12 November 1984.

Pugneys Country Park opened in 1985.

In May 1986, 158 acres at Wintersett, which had been the site of opencast coalmining, was opened by the West Yorkshire authority as Anglers' Country Park.

The site of Woolley Colliery became a country park in the 1990s. A length of the disused Barnsley Canal runs through it. There are several lakes and many footpaths. In the spring there are masses of cowslips and one can also find some coltsfoot as well as many other meadow flowers. Walking there is some small compensation for the sadness I feel at other changes and is not a bad thing to be able to do in one's seventies.

The monument in memory of Councillor Henry Daley erected in the 1990s at Walton Country Park. *The author*

CONCLUSION

Wakefield in the early years of the twenty first century is very different from the Wakefield I knew in my childhood. The slums are gone, but the drive for new housing today is to serve commuters to Leeds rather than people whose work lies in the town. Much of the employment base in coalmining, engineering and textiles has gone too. The sprawling industrial estates and office parks on the perimeter now help to sustain the economy but add little of attraction to the landscape. The town centre is heralded, on its main roads, by bland glass car showrooms. The once familiar and distinctive skyline of the city, with the Town Hall tower, the County Hall dome, and the Cathedral spire standing out, has become cluttered with high-rise flats.

The character of Wakefield – its individuality – is being eroded. It owed much to the developments in the eighteenth and nineteenth centuries which brought not only the handsome terraces of St John's and South Parade, but the group of civic buildings in Wood Street and the fine commercial properties in Westgate. The great classical Corn Exchange, which dominated Westgate for more than a century, is long gone. Since the abolition of the Quarter Sessions in 1971, the imposing Court House has fallen into a sorry state although its rehabilitation as part of the leisure industry has been promised.

I can think of no new building of the last half century that has that 'landmark' quality that gives a place its uniqueness.

The increasing popularity of family history reflects the importance of having roots. But for me roots mean place as well as people. The place provides the context for the rough times as well as the good ones. If I have had some bad experiences in Wakefield, I have also found immense interest in finding out more, and writing, about this place where I was born and have lived for more than seventy years, in particular its social and cultural history. I wonder what future local historians will have to say about a Wakefield influenced by somewhat remote bodies like Yorkshire Forward and in danger of being no more than a satellite of Leeds.

Perhaps there is a chance that Wakefield will regain both character and prestige in particular from art and drama. The Yorkshire

Sculpture Park, the proposed Waterfront Gallery, the budding trend for public sculptures like the conceptual stick of rhubarb erected on the edge of the park in 2005, bring some promise. Public Arts began and has remained in Wakefield. There are plans for the Art House – a complex of artists' studios – to be built in Drury Lane close to the Theatre Royal and Opera House. The theatre itself is to be extended.

When I began this book, I had Henry Clarkson's *Memories of Merry Wakefield* (1887) in mind. Towards the end of his account, Clarkson says,

> *A very warm feeling for my native place fills my mind … and I trust that firm friends and true will always be found to stand by her, and that brighter days even than any she has seen, may dawn and continue over her.*

Despite my criticisms, I share Clarkson's 'warm feeling' and I hope that something of Wakefield will live in my pages as it does in his. But I am not at all sure that his trust will prove well-founded!

The Rhubarb sculpture by Graeme Ritchie and Scot Fletcher. *The author*